T0198618

Adolf Hitler: Religionist

Naziism as a genuine religion

VERUS AMERICANUS

iUniverse, Inc.
New York   Bloomington

Adolf Hitler: Religionist
Naziism as a genuine religion

iUniverse books may be ordered through booksellers or by contacting:

iUniverse
1663 Liberty Drive
Bloomington, IN 47403
www.iuniverse.com
1-800-Authors (1-800-288-4677)

ISBN: 978-1-4401-3660-3 (sc)
ISBN: 978-1-4401-3665-8 (ebook)

Printed in the United States of America

iUniverse rev. date: 12/29/2009

Contents

1.	Introduction	vii
2.	Foreword	xi
3.	Chapter 1 – The Importance of the Childhood Years	1
4.	Chapter 2 – The Hitler Philosophy: Historical Beginnings	9
5.	Chapter 3 – The Hitler World View	20
6.	Chapter 4 – Creation of the Nazi Religion	39
7.	Chapter 5 – Nazi Mind Conditioning	45
8.	Chapter 6 – The Neanderthal Component	51
9.	Chapter 7 – The Nazi Religion: Institutionalization	61
10.	Chapter 8 – Modern Religion and Naziism: The Obvious Parallels	80

note: [ ] indicates author's comments

Introduction

The writing of a book of the type and implication that follows this introduction is a weighty task. Such an examination involves the author in a search for truth that attacks many of the psychological and philosophical fundamentals that have served as the bases of American society, at least since the setting of the Atlantic seaboard in the 1600s, and of European society from the time of St. Augustine or before.

It is never a popular action to attack any society's cherished system of beliefs, especially when those beliefs consist of some of the most emotional, fear generating, and generally passion provoking tenets that modern human beings possess in their cognitive makeups. Such investigations always create angry responses, and explicit denials by those "true believers", many of whom both historically and today seem to be willing to sacrifice their wealth, their well-being, and even their very lives to that system of thinking with which they were mind-conditioned as children. The importance of making such an investigation is, however, magnified when one observes the egregious errors and falsehoods in these beliefs and the enormous amount of human suffering and premature death that has resulted therefrom over at least the last 2000 years, of forced application, in contradiction to the basic nature of the human being.

This effort ranges in geography from the Far East to North America, in society from the poorest of the poor to the wealthy elitist, and philosophically from the most ignorant slave to individuals represented by someone as well anointed as Immanuel Kant. Untold human slaughter has followed these malignant ideas over geography, through time, and throughout entire societies where the psychological and philosophical errors have been institutionalized and forced on an unwilling public. In an era when the creation of weapons of mass destruction have, for the first time, allowed Mankind literally to destroy itself, all men of good will should make every effort to do what they can to right the wrongs that cause both political leaders and common men to act as their own destroyers. The time seem late to effect such fundamental changes in human thought; but change they must if the earth is not to be handed over, finally, to the insects and the fish.

Adolf Hitler

The adolescent that became Adolf Hitler was not a normal human child – neither physically nor psychologically. He was a sickly child, evidently from his birth on 20 April 1889, later developed into a monorchid, and received the dubious attentions of a worried and doting mother from the very beginning.

Klara (Polzl) Hitler, Adolf's mother, had led a precarious early life, being born into the grinding poverty of rural life along the border area between Germany and Austria near Braunau am Inn, in the late 19th Century. She married Alois Hitler, Adolf's father, in January of 1885, when she was 25 and he was 48. Alois and Klara were uncle and niece, and required Papal dispensation to legitimatize the wedding. The fruits of this marriage were evidently not genetically beneficial and Klara's first three children all died before the age of three years, and all from a poor resistance to the disease diphtheria – the last (Otto) in 1887. When Adolf was born in 1889, Klara was terrified that the sickly baby would soon join his three earlier siblings in the graveyard. Her excessive attention to the child was complexed by what the author believes to be a defensive withdrawal of the normal state of intimacy that develops between a mother and baby, to the point that the psychological nourishment required for a normal early development of the child was missing.

The author believes that the threat of the intense psychological pain of the loss of still another baby caused Klara to remain personally, intimately distant from this new child, while justifying this action (to herself) by a countervailing overprotection. Klara protected Adolf the very best she could from external threats (later to include her husband's violent temper) but, unknowingly, deprived him of that maternal closeness that is required to prevent a child from maturing into an overly self-centered, narcissistic individual who may come to believe that the world owes him a living and he should not be subjected to the rigors of the reality he is forced to live within.

This psychological phenomenology is well known in the annals of psychiatric pathology. The fact that the father (Alois) often beat the son (Adolf) viciously and on an almost daily basis, would strongly reinforce the son's belief that he was being unfairly treated by the facts of reality around him, was owed a debt by society as a result, and could not be charged with guilt if he demanded payment for that debt. In observing the important, informative elements of the development of the child, Adolf Hitler, the author cannot imagine a better suited early environment for the formation of the narcissistic, self-justified, and hate-filled adult that became Adolf Hitler, the Fuhrer of the Nazis, and then all of Germany.

Historical Social Waves

The author makes the proposal that 1930s National Socialism in Germany was, fundamentally, the result of a "chaotic social wave," (taken in close, causative analogy to the well-known "rogue sea-wave" – the bane of all seafarers and the source of the story of the modern motion picture, *The Poseidon Adventure*), beginning to form (in modern times) in the early 1800s, with Fichte, von Kleist, and Jahn – accelerating in the following years through Nietzsche, Hegel, and the Grimm brothers – and receiving great sustenance in the Second Reich with Paul deLagarde, Julius Langbehn, Max Weber, and Wilhelm Marr. The failure of a nascent democratic movement at the time of the Revolution of 1848 (in hindsight) destroyed any possibility of limiting this growing chaotic social development, which easily survived the trauma of 1918 and reached its peak in the 1933/38 time period in the melding of the horribly warped Hitler persona with the now overpowering tidal surge of the extreme German nationalist identification. Together they (Adolf Hitler and the now cresting social chaotic waveform) constructively interfered to maximize the result in earth shaking reverberations, peaking physically and psychologically with the assault on European civilization in WW II, and the state sponsored murder of human beings on an unbelievable scale – both foreign and German. National Socialism as practiced in the Third Reich is unimaginable without the fuhrer that was Adolf Hitler, operating in accordance with the "Fuhrerprincip" in a German society prepared by 150 years of philosophical development supporting a hatred of reason as a principle, and an organized program of looting via conquest as a method of national income. The social chaotic waveform peaked under the guidance of Adolf Hitler to create the world-wide historical disaster that was WW II. The philosophy was German Romanticism. Its (social) metaphysics was German mythology, its epistemology was the *Fuhrerprincip*, its politics was totalitarian militarism, and its ethics, egalitarian racism. There was very little room in the romanticism of National Socialism for reason, and no room at all for the morality of individual human rights.

The playing out of this 20th Century horror story is one that has been researched and explained from seemingly every possible standpoint since 1945, and even before. The author believes that, in this work, he has made observations and correlations that have not been well-covered in the past, and that the conditions and the psychological and societal fundamentals that allowed the elevation of the Adolf Hitler of the 1930s and 1940s may be developing, still again, in the early 21st Century. If this is so, surely it can be argued that things MUST change.

Foreword

On January 20, 1933, Adolf Hitler entered the Presidential Palace where the President of the Weimar Republic, Paul von Hindenburg appointed him to the political position of Chancellor of the Republic. In the parliamentary system of the Weimar government, this position (while of considerable political power) was one that could be theoretically quite limited in its independent effect on government operations by the placement of a majority (8 to 2) of circumscribing cabinet members with different ideas. This office was somewhat similar to that of the COO (Chief Operating Officer) of a very large modern American corporation, and was crowded around with a number of other politicians who would be able to exert a controlling effect on the decisions and actions of the man in the Chancellorship – or so they thought. The political intrigue that resulted in this appointment is both complicated and stultifying even to those German politicians of a mind of political immediacy, who should have known something of the character of the man being appointed. The political and personal arrogance and gross egotism of Franz von Papen, Alfred Hugenberg, General Kurt von Schleicher, and others could not make up for the bumbling incompetence of the dottering old von Hindenburg, whose intellectual and political perspicuity (to the extent he ever possessed it) had evaporated into senility for more than a decade into the past. Dealing with Hitler they were as a fold of sheep faced with a devouring wolf (and this is exactly how Hitler saw himself) in the field of the *realpolitik* of the time. Hitler bowed and scraped to the old field marshal to get the appointment he so craved, and the limits of Hindenburg's judgement and the conservative circumscription were immediately exceeded.

On February 22, 1933, less than 30 days into the new administration, Hermann Goering appointed 55,000 members of Hitler's private, paramilitary National Socialists, the Sturm-Abteilung (SA) bully boys as auxiliary police, and their formerly illegal terror tactics now became legal, government sanctioned actions. On February 27, 1933, the Nazis set fire to the analog of the American Capitol Building, the German Reichstag, and immediately began inciting the politicians and the public for the power to protect the German people from the Communist insurrection, which they blamed for starting the fire. The immediate results of this program of power consolidation was the Enabling Act passed by the Reichstag on March 24, which (after Hindenburg's "Decree for the Protection of the German Nation" on February 4) made Hitler a de facto political dictator. At about this time the concentration camps (an effective innovation borrowed by an admiring Hitler from V.I. Lenin and Josef Stalin of the Soviet Union) were constructed and began to be filled with all those who disagreed with Hitler's version of German nationalism. This would continue until 1945.

For a number of years Hitler had had direct control of the most powerful "private" army in Germany in the SA and the Schutzstaffel (SS), and, since several German states already had National Socialist governments, the new elections called for March 5, 1933, sounded a death-knell for any state resistance or *federalism* applied against the central government in Berlin. With complete control of the news media, and especially the new technology of radio, in a remarkably short time Hitler had gained a level of political power that was seriously limited only by the person of von Hindenburg, himself. It took over a year for Mother Nature to aid Hitler in discarding that particular limitation, when Hindenburg died on August 2, 1934. Only one short day *earlier*, Hitler had caused a decree to be made that combined the political offices of Chancellor and President in himself. Two days later, the German military were forced to swear allegiance not to Germany or even the Weimar constitution, but to Adolf Hitler, personally. At this point in time, Hitler had achieved absolute (totalitarian) power in Germany, subject only to the possibility of being murdered, or being arrested by the still powerful German military.

Thus, it came to pass that one of the most twisted, immoral, and perverted individual human beings of his day managed to become absolute dictator over a nation state composed of the single most inventive, hardworking, and creative nation state of people on the face of the globe. How this happened is a wondrous and convoluted story, but it one with which we of the 21st Century must become intimately familiar, or else history will surely repeat itself, and result, finally, in the greatest destruction of human life the world has ever seen.

CHAPTER 1

The Importance of the Childhood Years

Adolf Hitler was born on April 20, 1889, in the town of Braunau, Austria, on the Inn river. Thus, Hitler was not born German, but Austrian. The importance of this, his place of birth, cannot be over stressed. The later failure of the German court to deport him back to Austria after the failed Munich putsch of 1923, and his time in prison (as specified by the law), would ultimately facilitate all that happened in Germany, at his instigation, thereafter.

The Religious Contribution

The society in which Hitler, the child, was raised was one that was steeped in the religion of Martin Luther, and the necessity of all good Lutherans to love and obey the minions of the state, almost unconditionally. In keeping with the fundamental tenets of the Christian religion generally, the society was one that looked upon human sexuality as something that unfortunately all men possessed, should try to live down as best they could, and was certainly not considered as anything of exceptional moral value in the range of elevated human characteristics. The result was that Adolf, the child, was ill prepared to personally witness the actions of a cruel father whose sexual appetites included the quasi-rape of his mother before his very eyes. The fact that his mother seemed to (finally) appreciate the action associated with the rape, was something with which an ill-prepared child could not deal in a psychologically healthy manner.

For some very good reasons, the pubescent Hitler grew up as a sexually and psychologically warped individual (much as many

1

evangelical Christians in this country) whose sexual aberrations would turn ever more to the exotic and twisted nature of the true sexual pervert. Partially, because of an inordinate fear of the normal human sexual relationship between man and woman, he would not marry until the last few hours of his life, and his view of a normal sex life, centered around vaginal intercourse, was something he abhorred. He had considerable homosexual fears that were well founded, even though he apparently did not consciously accept the homosexual activities, requirements, or lifestyle in any important way. The work of the Christian society (and his parents) in distorting the basic nature of the human being, in the child and boy who was Adolf Hitler, had done their work well. He would be sexually warped until he died as a suicide, and his aberrated learning about his sexuality and the normal and proper tolerant frame of mind in his relationship to other human beings would be transformed into a virulent aggression against the world, at large.

This came about as a result of his sexual pecularities mixed with a firm belief in various ancient Teutonic myths of the type Richard Wagner, the composer and philosopher, presented in his operas dealing with the uniqueness and greatness of the German culture when it was combined with strong Lutheran (and Catholic) religious elements of obedience to the will of the leaders of a strong state apparatus. Hitler consciously, selectively, and specifically fulfilled the expectations of the model of these great, historical figures touted by German myth for a hundred years or more, who were to lead the German people to world domination as nature's "chosen people." The smallness and meanness of the very intellectually limited individual who would finally become the totalitarian leader of the Third Reich was not expected by the artists and philosophers of the 19th Century who prepared the way for Hitler in the German culture. To them such a leader would simply have to be the virtual reincarnation of Frederick the Great, or some autarkist similitude, Hitler, the man, would have been viewed by them (and by the overwhelming majority in 1930s Germany had they truly known him) as a vagabond and an uneducated and crude dolt. The truth of history is that in a government organization prepared by the outstanding men of the mind (good *or* bad), these men are almost never those who manage to actually gain political power in the government institutions they so carefully prepared. This has happened in the America of the 1780s and the 1850s, and it also happened in the Germany of the 1920s.

The Family Contribution

The child, Adolf Hitler, had a built-in love/hate relationship with his parents that was not of his own doing. His stern and egotistic father beat him on a daily basis and his mother did what she could to protect the youngster from the worst of her husband's temper. Her protection naturally gravitated to over-protection and (later) doting, due to the fact that she had already lost three children to disease. This love/hate situation forced on a child by his parents results in a well recognized psychological syndrome known to cause introversion and arrested development. When the cruelty component of the syndrome is extreme (there was at least once when Adolf's father feared his beating had killed the boy), the surviving ego does and must turn strongly to a defensive posture. Part and parcel of this posture is, of course, introversion; but in extremeus, the tortured ego lashes out at his persecutor and any entity or entities to which the role of "torturer" is psychologically transferred. In the case of Aldof Hitler, this transference would ultimately apply to Marxists and Jews, many of whom (disgracefully for Jews) were one and the same. When the early-established mental aberrations of Adolt Hitler, the child, were empowered by political means in Hitler, the developmentally arrested dictator, a coordinated and far-ranging system of "pay back" resulted against Marxists (both Communists and Social Democrats) and Jews that would shake and horrify the entire world – even the unbelievably monstrous leadership of Nazi Germany's major socialist competitor in the world, the Union of Soviet Socialist Republics, Communist Russia.

The Education Contribution

The state sponsored system that furnished the early education of the boy, Adolf Hitler and his captive comrades, was neither passive nor faultless in the development of Adolf Hitler, the driving force of the Nazi Party of the 1920s, and the dictator of Germany for the long and terrible 12 years that the highly touted Thousand Year Reich actually lasted.

The exposure of the boy, Hitler, to the government education system was *somewhat* limited, simply because he was such a poor student. He was asked to leave the Linz high school in 1904, but things did not materially improve when he entered the Realschule at Steyr, a small neighboring industrial town. In her book, *Hitler's Vienna*, Brigitte Hamann quotes Hitler (in 1942) on page 19 as saying, "At thirteen, fourteen, fifteen I no longer believed in anything, certainly none of my friends still believed in the so-called communion, only a few totally stupid honor students ! Except, at the time I thought everything should be blown up." Such a quotation (if truly stated) is a strong indication that this teenager had no care for commonly accepted religion, and that the natural sort of rebellion present in most pubescents was present in the boy at a level much higher than "natural." This, in itself, is an indication of a strong psychological transference of the learned hate he felt for his (now deceased) father to the authority figures he found around him – including the state itself. This would later show up especially strongly during his years in Vienna.

Hamann further states on page 19, "With three unsatisfactory grades – in German, math, and stenography – Hitler was again kept back. [Hitler said] *This idiot of a professor spoiled the German language for me, this bungling pathetic gnome: I would never be able to write a proper letter! Imagine! With a D minus from that buffoon, I could have never become a technician.*"

The obvious purpose of this quotation is to blame the system and the people running the system. It is (from this distance in time) hard to fault the professor of German who, "....spoiled the German language for me, ..." since Hitler would never in his life use the language as an educated or even normally cultured man. At this time Hitler supposedly succumbed to a "serious lung disease" which allowed him to leave the unhappy and demeaning environment of the Steyer school and rejoin his doting (and non-threatening mother in Linz. The author believes this event was nothing less than the 15 year old not being willing to "stick it out" in an intellectual situation that was difficult for him; in other words, he quit and used a feigned illness as his excuse.

The Early Social Contribution

The contribution of the society in which young Hitler lived to his moral and emotional development effectively started in the town in which he attended school since the year 1900 – Linz, the provincial capital. Now, any youngster of age eleven is not going to be interested in things political, at least in a serious way. Things political involve keen interpersonal relationships and a certain maturity of understanding. But there is no doubt that the boy was subjected to the talk, the printed news, and the personal push-and-shove that was endemic in the Linz high school and town. The Hapsburg Empire was beginning to come apart and the politics and sociology of both "free thinkers" and German nationalists in the larger towns of Austria were loud and sometimes belligerent. As time passed and Adolf achieved the advanced age of fifteen, the political awareness and the emotional commitment to social ideals began to gel in his young mind. Hamann quotes Hitler as saying," ....I again heard a song of my youth. Once upon a time I sang it so often with a heart full of belief, that proud battle song: "Das Volk steht auf, der Sturm bricht los" (The people are rising up, the storm is breaking loose)."

The desire of a pubescent boy to "belong" is great. For an introverted Adolf Hitler, in the social tumult that was Linz in the time from 1900 to 1904, the social pressure to be a member of some group or another must have been irresistible. The group that was closest to a "grass roots" movement that would appeal to an unsophisticated young man was pan-German and "folkish" nationalism. In any case loyalty to the Hapsburg dynasty required loyalty to the Hapsburg state, a multicultural view of social organization, and an international view of the incorporation of diverse social and political human groups. Even mature men, well versed in politics, could easily agree that the Hapsburg Empire, as constituted in 1904, was a nonviable entity that should be recognized or simply disappear from the world stage. On page 17 Hamann quotes Hitler as saying, "....I lived my youth enmeshed in the border struggle for German language, culture, and thought, of which the great majority of the German people had no idea during peacetime. Even when I was thirteen, that fight incessantly pushed itself on us, and it was fought in every high school class." At least to this point in time the young Adolf Hitler was not an anti-Semite and showed no signs of becoming one. Hamann says on page 23, "When in 1938 an emissary of the NSDAP archive collected biographical material on the "Fuhrer" in Linz, he learned much to his amazement that 'funnily enough' Hitler's favorite actors in Linz – that is to say, his Wagner and Schiller heroes – were 'almost exclusively Jews.'" At this time the young man evidently appreciated artistic talent above all, and Jews, generally, are the single most talented genotypical group of people on the earth.

The Vienna Contribution

In 1905 Hitler (while still in Linz) met a young man about his own age, August Kubizek, at an opera theater. This source yields insight into the effect of Wagner's music on young Hitler, as well as Hitler's later Vienna response to a contemporary who *was* successful in his artistic endeavors. Hitler's very emotional response to the opera, *Tienzi*, was formative in his self-view and the life's path and vocation he later chose for himself. Hamann says on page 24, "After the opera, Kubizek later wrote, sixteen-year-old Hitler walked with him in a "totally transported state" to Linz's Frein Mountain until the early hours of the morning." Existing to a large degree in his own mind, the boy would orate to the mountains and the trees and rocks. It seems that he was attempting to communicate directly with nature, in a personal manner. The author believes this to be a desperate effort by the teenager's subconscious to be recognized – an attempt to establish the psychological visibility he did not find at home and in only one boyhood friend, August Kubicek. Hitler allegedly stated to the Kubizek family that he wanted "... to become a people's tribune," much as Cola di Reinzi did in Wagner's opera, and actually did historically in 14th Century Italy. The intensely dynamic and emotional overture to the opera would be used by Hitler as an "opening piece" to the ceremonies starting the yearly Nuremberg Nazi Party meetings. Hamann also says on page 24,

> Young Hitler's manner of speaking, Kubizek noted, was "very choice." In other words, contrary to those around him, he did not speak a dialect but High German. In addition he had a "well-developed sense of performing." The young man

displayed his desire to be the center of attention by being given to talking much and persistently, always in the form of monologues. He did not permit anyone to contradict him. "Sometimes, when he became entirely lost in his fantasies, I got the suspicion that everything he said was nothing but oratory."

The author proposes that Hitler's strong tendency to force his attention on others, and his even stronger desire to be the center of attention was a learned trait from his father's autocratic nature combined with an inferiority complex from failures in his father's expectations. He may not have had any love for his father, but he certainly had respect and fear. Fear is an emotion that is as easy to learn and emulate as is love. This syndrome would be reinforced by his twice repeated failure to gain entrance into the Vienna art school, and developed even more powerfully as he aged and his bitterness turned into a powerful hate projected against the city and anyone who disagreed with him. Vienna was a natural for an artist of even modest ability, but its "rejection" of him created, finally, a hatred that would be acted out immediately after the anschluss in 1938.

Hitler's artistic nature and the world famous art center that was Vienna were things that the young man could not keep apart, and in May of 1906, seventeen year old Adolf Hitler arrived in Vienna for the first time - a visit of some two weeks or so. In this visit Adolf witnessed a performance of *Tristan* by conductor Gustav Mahler, which must have impressed the young man to an extraordinary depth. After the visit, Hamann quotes Kubizek on page 27, "In his thoughts he frequently was no longer in Linz but was already living right in the center of Vienna."

In October of 1906, Hitler started taking piano lessons from Kubizek's teacher, in an effort to become more musically educated and knowledgeable, like his friend. This effort was no more successful with his personal abilities than was his artistic effort at drawing/painting. But in January of 1907 there started a fundamental change in Adolf's life when his mother was diagnosed with breast cancer. The disease would progress with ever greater effect until she died of its ravages on 21 December 1907. In the meantime the son's infatuation with Vienna had only increased and he persuaded his mother to allow him to try to enter the Vienna art school in the fall. His first try to be admitted in September/October of 1907 was not successful and his second try in September of 1908 even less so.

In February of 1908, Adolf convinced Kubizek to come to Vienna to study music and keep him company in his artistic endeavors. But Kubizek's success in his field of music grated on Hitler's nerves, as a strong and present contrast with his failure in his own artistic field. In November of 1908 Hitler left his Vienna residence with no word of his relocation to an absent Kubizek. When Kubizek returned (from a spate of working for his father in Linz and military training) to Vienna later that month, Hitler was nowhere to be found. Hitler's very fragile ego could not stand the comparison, but he had learned *something* from his stay in the capital. He had learned how to organize and stage an operatic drama – something he would put to good use in the "theater" of the yearly Nuremberg November conventions of the Nazi Party in the 1930s.

CHAPTER 2

The Hitler Philosophy: Historical Beginnings

The child, Adolf Hitler, was no more philosophically minded than any other 6 year old boy, but the circumstances under which he was raised were such that his surroundings were less attractive to him than the world within his own mind. The fact that the boy, Adolf, was an introverted child is without question, and is covered in detail in chapters 1 and 4 of this book. But the fact of his introversion, and its expansion into his teenage years, was instrumental in the incorporation of the unusual and extreme views of the world and society he encountered in the cosmopolitan metropolis that was Vienna, Austria.

The introvert is a natural for accepting the idea that living in society results in a process of "us against them." This is especially true when the "us" consists of a group of rural, uneducated people of poor means, and the "them" consists of a group of city dwelling, sophisticates of relative wealth, many of whom seemed strange (the Jews) and even threatening to a small town youth. For a period at the age of around 15, Adolf attempted to understand and even befriend selected Viennese Jews around him; but it did not take long for him to discern that *he* was the outsider, would remain that way, and was, in addition, looked down upon as someone not quite socially equal. For Adolf, the teenager, "us against them" transformed into "me against them." The importance of this early metamorphosis cannot be overemphasized.

The author observes that Jews are the most intelligent and talented single group of people on the earth (see further commentary in Chapter 6) and they do, unfortunately, sometimes come across as appearing to think themselves superior to other people. The boy, Adolf, did experience this attitude, as did many others in the Austro-Hungarian Empire, and all across Europe. Even thought he started out in Vienna as a pro-Semite, he slowly acquired the anti-Semitism that would remain with him and only grow stronger as he aged. This came to him by means of unfortunate personal experiences with Jews, and accepting as fact the writings of numerous racial and cultural demagogues from Richard Wagner to Gustave Le Bon. Some of these comtemporaris were not satisfied with "live and let live" and endeavored to arrange things politically, so that the Jew would be put in his place. The ignorant and malleable young man that was Adolf Hitler fell victim to this sort of thinking, the consequences of which would become horrible beyond imagining to any contemporary Viennese citizen of 1910.

Early Teachers

Any young man, especially a young, introverted individual with a great amount of personal drive perceives the world around as would an intellectual sponge – eager to absorb – eager to learn and build. The Hapsburg Empire had been great for a long time, and the ideas, the people, and the talent that naturally migrated to the seat of that empire, Vienna, were the most creative and most outstanding the times had to offer. The city that had showcased the great Mozart and the phenomenal Beethoven had attracted civil engineers who constructed the Ringstrasse and architects who constructed its majestic buildings. The Vienna Art School (The Academy of Visual Arts) was renown throughout Europe and the population was quite diverse, extremely interesting, and inordinately able. To a young, impressionable teenager from the Austrian outback, the cosmopolitan ambiance had to be overwhelming. Surely, he thought, this was a place where one who wanted so much to learn and belong could start to make his mark on history. But wanting was not enough. Adolf Hitler had grown up (thanks to a doting mother) expecting the world and success would fall into his arms. He simply had not learned that to accomplish great deeds and to be accepted into the companionship of great men required great talent and a large amount of hard work.

The boy, Adolf, did not possess the former and was, with the latter, unwilling.

He had made his application to the Vienna Art School and sent in his drawings and paintings, and he was waiting, in great expectation, for a resounding welcome. In the meantime he was directing his attention to the local intellectual culture as best he could, with the performing arts, lectures and discussions, and the quasi-subculture that lurks in the cafes and beer houses of every dynamic city. Heroes, as life examples, are important to young men. The only true, historical hero for young Adolf was the composer/philosopher Richard Wagner. In this man he discovered a composer of music of a kind and emotional content that ensnares all those who become initiates. This, together with the Teutonic Wagnerian operatic themes enraptured young Adolf to the point of enslavement, not only to the emotional content of the incredible music but also with the emotional content of the writing of Wagner, the philosopher. The strong anti-Semitism of Wagner enforced by the even more intense anti-Semitism of Theodor Fritsch, Guido von List, Georg Lanz von Liebenfels, and even Vienna Mayor Dr. Karl Leuger (from whom Hitler gleaned much of his appreciation of, and belief in, the power of oratory), led the eager young mind to a condition from which an inordinate hatred of Jews would develop. This happened, in spite of the fact that in his early Vienna years Hitler counted many Jews as admired persons and even friends and helpers. The fact that the Jewish physician, Dr. Eduard Bloch, who tended Adolf's mother at the time of her death was specially favored by Hitler, the dictator, is a matter of historical record. But Jew hatred would become, for National Socialism, an important component in its philosophical accommodation; and this was just as true in the Germany of the 1930s as it now is in the Arabic Middle East of 2009.

A Personal Philosophy

Every individual human being has a personal philosophy. If one chooses to frequent any number of "midnight main streets" in virtually any town across the United States (or the rest of the earth) the dregs of the local society will be there to observe. If one chooses to strike up conversations with an average member of any of these groups, one will quickly discover that there are some who have never heard of the term, philosophy, very few who can even speak to its meaning, and probably none will admit to being philosophically minded. Yet when questioned about their reasons for doing the last series of things they did, they will respond with reasoning explanations. When asked about thoughts they have about this thing or that thing, they respond straightforwardly and usually in a reasonably rational manner. They will continue to do this, sometimes taking a small period for reflection before answering, but *not always* providing evidence for prior rationality. They will continue to do this, with great variance in individual opinion, depending on the topic, until they start to tire of the whole exercise. At that point in time the trained psychologist can usually pretty well "type" the individuals he has talked with, and begin to predict their responses to selected questions. The psychologist has then established a rough determination of their thought patterns and the bases upon which their mental decisions and physical actions are made. In terms that would be unintelligible to all but a few of any such grouping, the psychologist would have made a partial identification of the *life philosophies* of these individuals.

When the group of people so examined by our psychologist, above, is switched to the average man-on-the-street, very little changes. He will find a few more who have heard of the term, philosophy, and a few more who can speak to the term with some understanding, but few (if any) who understand what they are speaking to.

The next group in line for our psychologist are those with a college level education. In this group, unless they are technically oriented, one will begin to find more people who understand some of the basics of the concept of philosophy and are sometimes actually able to make cogent definitions of philosophical terms. Only when the examined group is restricted to those who have made a serious study of the history of Man and the workings of the human mind, will our psychologist come upon those who start to recognize the importance of philosophy to human lives. But even among this very select group one will discover a large percentage who do not accept or understand that every human being who has ever lived (assuming compos mentis) possesses a life's philosophy that he has chosen to live by.

A philosophy, any philosophy, is composed of three main components – metaphysics, epistemology, and ethics. Other areas that are normally considered "philosophical" in nature, such as art and politics, are derivative concepts – important, but derivative. When the well-informed, serious student of the human condition first makes a critical examination of his own philosophy, he carefully and judiciously examines all the elements of the three fundamental philosophical components. This examination involves a detailed identification of all these elements in accordance with the most rigorous application of reason of which he is capable. The elements are weighed for veridicality and order of importance and placed into the (mental) hierarchical set in which they best fit. This then becomes the individual's personal philosophy – *an open-ended concept.* This quick and cursory sketch by the author, of the "examined life" should, in the mentally healthy human being, continue on a permanent basis, for as long as one lives.

The process so described is not the usual way in which an individual's personal philosophy is constructed. Indeed, except for the very small number of people described in the paragraph above, the elements of the individual's personal philosophy in metaphysics, epistemology, and ethics are accepted into an individual's mind, almost, non-critically – many times, simply because someone told him something to believe. The ordinary person tends to accept things from his social and physical environment by the method of happenstance – whatever he sees or hears that "sounds right" or makes him "feel good". It sometimes seems to the author that the all-important, life-critical philosophical components of the average man are acquired from his surroundings by a social method approximating the chemical process of *osmosis.* The author also observes that no where else in the realm of human endeavor is so little attention and effort paid to something of such extreme and paramount importance as the construct of the individual human philosophy by the average person.

And yet, the most false and poorly examined personal philosophy is commonly accepted as just as effective as the most true and rigorously examined personal philosophy in subsuming and driving the subject's life and attaining his life's goals. When Adolf Hitler, the teenaged boy, found himself in the grand and overwhelming seat of the Austro-Hungarian Empire, Vienna, he possessed the sponge-like mentality and the youthful drive of the young man, desiring to succeed, but none of the mental equipment necessary to examine and control that which entered his mind and those things he chose to accept as his own – to accept as truth. He did not have this equipment because he did not receive the training to have it – neither at home nor at school. *In this sense*, he was the victim of his environment, and the chaotic social wave that continued to build in Germany swept the young man, Adolf Hitler, along, until it crested in the year 1933, with Adolf Hitler, the dictator, riding the crest.

Richard Wagner

On page 99 of his book, **The Psychopathic God, Adolf Hitler**, Robert Waite, says, "It is very difficult to exaggerate the importance of Wagner in Hitler's life and thought. He himself best summarized that influence when he said that anyone who sought to understand him and his movement should first understand Richard Wagner."

Of course what Waite is describing when he refers to "Hitler's life and thought" is, more fundamentally simply the results of his personal philosophy. The extraordinary importance Hitler placed on the influence of Wagner in his life and the parallel influence of writers and speakers available to him in Vienna, was a formative and formidable intellectual driving force that captured the functioning of the young and limited psyche of the boy, Adolf, that remained solid and virtually inflexible to the very hour of his death. The combination of the "us against them" anti-Semitism of Wagner combined with a quality of music capable of causing in the listener what can only be properly described as an *emotional orgasm* was something irresistible to the eager young mind. Hitler's intellectual perspicuity was limited, but his *will be believe* in a philosophical essence that supported his ego and accepted him as a full-fledged member was not.

In the very next paragraph Waite says,

> Adolf's boyhood swung around the pole of Wagner. "My youthful enthusiasm for the Master of Bayreuth," he recalled later, "knew no bounds." As his only friend of those years

noted, "Listening to Wagner meant to him not a visit to the theatre, but the opportunity of being transported into the extraordinary state which Wagner's music produced in him, that escape into a mystical dream world which he needed in order to endure the tensions of his turbulent nature . . . . He was intoxicated and bewitched . . . ."

When one finds apparent egoistic acceptance by someone as artistically and historically powerful as Richard Wagner, the swelling of the self esteem is quickly followed by a strong desire to become active and important in the movement of ideas which have become so critical to one's life. There are very few who do not want to be the "hero" in a group or movement that is so important to them. Adolf Hitler, the young man of 1910, dreamed of becoming a contemporary Lohengrin somehow, sometime in the future. Adolf Hitler, the unquestioned leader of the Nazi Party in 1923, had convinced himself (and many others) that he *was* a modern Lohengrin of the German people and reinforced the idea at every turn. Waite tells us on page 101 of his book.

Hitler cherished all Wagner's operas, but both as a young man in Vienna and as chancellor, his favorite was probably Lohengrin. He saw it at least ten times in Vienna, and as chancellor he amazed opera buffs with the fact that he knew the entire libretto by heart. . . . Let it be suggested here (and discussed in detail later) that Hitler preferred Lohengrin to all other operas chiefly because he saw himself as the immaculate knight who rescued his beloved young mother (both Klara Hitler and the German Motherland) from his lecherous and race-contaminating old father, who had been, in point of fact, the legal guardian of Klara before he married her. It does not seem a mere coincidence that in 1938, Hitler approved of a portrait of himself as Sir Adolf, a flashing-eyed, stern-visaged knight in shining armor and Charlie Chaplin mustache astride a mighty stallion, the bearer of a new cross and the defender of a racially pure Germania. Of the dozens of portraits painted of the Fuhrer in 1938, Hitler chose this one as the official painting which alone was to be exhibited during the year.

That the Hitler philosophy contained a very large, even an overwhelming element of religious myth cannot be doubted. The torchlight parades, the beacon fires on hilltops, the Teutonic burial ceremony for President von Hindenburg (a staunch Catholic who had said he wanted no such ceremony), and especially the schools and training centers for the SS all exemplified the methodology that Hitler used to bring in and unite the German people into a society that would praise him as a hero and respond willingly to whatever he wished them to do. Hitler, himself, believed in this religious mythology without reservation. His acceptance of this system of belief started early in his life, in the Vienna years. On page 102 Waits says.

Hitler shared Wagner's infatuation with the mythical universe of primitive German legend. His two favorite books, which he read again and again as a youth in Vienna, were a volume on architecture and a popular edition of heroic legends entitled *Legends of Gods and Heroes: The Treasures of Germanic Mythology*. The Nordic mysteries that enthralled the boy continued to intrigue the man. . . . . [Hitler said] "When I hear Wagner it seem to me that I hear rhythms of a bygone world. I imagine to myself that one day science will discover in the waves set in motion by the *Rheingold*, secret mutual relations connected with the order of the world."

So it came to pass in 1933, that an intellectually limited, very unsophisticated human being named Adolf Hitler was legally appointed to lead the German people as *chief operating officer* (the German Chancellorship), and began to complete his own life's goal as being someone admired, someone feared, someone loved, someone important and historically remembered by a large group of dedicated and servile subjects. This came about as a result of chaotic social wave composed of separate elements the absence of even one of which occurring at just the same moment in time would probably have precluded the event. To restate, it is the author's opinion that the phenomenon of Adolf Hitler and all that meant to the world of the

20th Century would not have happened if the following events and conditions had not occurred when and as they did.

1. The philosophical preparation of the Germanic people to accept authoritative leadership and conformity from early in its modern history – starting with the horror of the Thirty Years War of 1618-1648, that literally depopulated large parts of the center of Germany.

2. The philosophical reinforcement of this mind-set in the German people by: Kant (a German) in limiting reason and preparing the way for Romanticism; Friedrich "Father" Jahn (a German) calling for a fanatic collectivist German nationalism and the fuhrer principle; and Wagner (a German) calling for a "Nordic" nationalism, an end to any sort of "capitalist" democracy, and a virulent anti-Semitism.

3. The end of WW I in de facto defeat, when the German army was still an army in being and was *not* overcome and destroyed in the field.

4. The Versailles Treaty that quite unnecessarily humiliated and impoverished the German people as a whole. Any "blame" for WW I could easily be divided among the countries and politicians of Russia, France, Serbia, Austria, Germany and even England.

5. The advent of the Bolshevik Revolution in Russia and the great fear generated by its almost immediate exportation to Germany. In November of 1932 the German Communist Party (KDP) was the third most powerful political party in Germany, just three percentage points behind the Social Democrats in the Reichstag.

6. The enormous financial and social destruction caused first by the run-away inflation of 1922-23, followed by the world-wide depression of the early 1930s. People were absolutely *desperate* for someone to take control of

things, and somehow to undo the damage that had been done to them.

7. The unwillingness of the Weimar government officials to militarily fight the Nazi menace when it was still weak, in the 1929-32 period.

8. The presence of Paul von Hindenburg in the Weimar presidency in the early 1930s – a political position in which this senile old man could wield dictatorial power for himself and others simply by declaring a national emergency, based on Articles 25 and 48 of the Reich Constitution.

9. The ability of the core of the Germans army to survive and stay together, even after Versailles and during the Weimar Republic. The importance of this fact was increased manyfold by the ability of that army to create new weapons and most importantly, develop revolutionary tactics and doctrine that would allow that army to strike faster and harder, and exploit enemy weakness to a degree not previously seen in history. To a great extent this was made possible by the efforts of an army officer named Heinz Guderian, whose efforts in communications, command, and control, especially with armored groups, was absolutely radical. Without this phenomenal new ability the army could not have accomplished what it did in 1939-40, Hitler would not have been in the political position in Europe that he was in the summer of 1940, and it is even probable that he would have been removed as head-of-state by the army in October or November of 1939.

It is true that these nine events/conditions are not all mutually independent, but it is also true that they all existed strongly and/or peaked in the 1930 to 1940 time period in a Germany whose leadership possessed an exalted opinion of its own ability, and an insufficient confidence in the ability of the ordinary German people to govern themselves without so much "leadership". The Hitler philosophy resonated strongly in many of the people in 1930-1932, even though essentially none of them understood Hitler's overwhelming desire to control and dictate, and his dedication to future war. This lack of understanding would extend into the summer of 1933, when it was much too late to remedy things in accordance with any democratic principles that still survived in the rapidly failing Weimar Republic. At this point in time WW II (and the Holocaust that resulted) was only a matter of time and circumstance.

CHAPTER 3

The Hitler World View

The world view of the Nazi organization of the 1920s and 1930s was predominately that of Adolf Hitler. This world view was a distillation of philosophical elements and psychological traits acquired by Hitler from about 1906 to about 1928, strongly colored and shaped by the learning and experiences of his formative years, starting around 1895. His world view was, virtually, total fantasy. This will be demonstrated in the following sections of this chapter, as will the underlying reason for that condition.

EARLY LEARNING

Psychologists believe that the most important and definite characteristics of the adult human being are rooted in the formative years, perhaps represented by that period from the age of 6 to 16. If something of importance is learned during this period (it is argued), that first learning will remain with the person throughout life, and contradictions to this learning will become extraordinarily difficult to accomplish. This generality held true for Adolf Hitler. The pain and humiliation he suffered at the hand of his cruel father resulted in a learned mind-set that would filter and shape his future learning, for the rest of his life. Psychologists tell us that psychological visibility of the human ego by others is necessary for that ego to develop in a manner that is *socially acceptable* or, in extremis, even to support survival. The boy, Adolf, had such visibility from his mother, who protected him as she could, but from no one else, in a personal manner, until he met August Kubicek in 1905. Adolf was 16 years old. But even the acceptance of Kubicek as someone providing psychological visibility was destroyed in Adolf's mind, when his success in the field

20

of music contrasted so strongly with his own abysmal failure in the field of the visual arts. After his second failure to enter the Vienna art school in September of 1908, Adolf could not stand the humiliation of facing his roommate again, and left their shared apartment in November with no forwarding address.

The now permanently warped psyche within Adolf Hitler would make itself more and more apparent as he aged. He had learned that having friends and loved ones resulted in psychological pain, and he simply resisted this in the future. This extended to friendships and relationships with females (in spite of the enormous sex drive of the teenager, fueled by run-away doses of hormones), when his great love of 1906, *Stefanie*, seemed to enjoy the company of handsome military lieutenants, to his exclusion. The fact that Stefanie never even knew he existed was immaterial in his mind. His belief, in the self-constructed mental world of the extreme introvert, that she had deserted him was taken as real. His later (apparently sexual) relationship with his niece, Angela Rabaul, resulted in her suicide (September 1931), so she had deserted him also, and he had been thoroughly infatuated with "Geli". (There is some reason to suspect that Geli was murdered by an unknown assailant(s).) He later married the only female companion who did not desert him, Eva Brown, who chose to die with him in the Fuhrer bunker in 1945.

His psyche would receive psychological visibility of a reliable quality only of a communicative type from the general public of Germany who composed the audiences for his speeches. His relationship with the crowds of his public talks can only be described as one of "mutual sustenance". The adoring and responsive public provided him with the psychological visibility he so craved, so that he forced a personally extremely tiring, highly emotional component into his speeches to receive the necessary recognition. He actually made as many as 10 speeches in a single day, receiving a public psychological approval that fueled his psyche much as heroin does for the addict. Notably, when he (rarely) addressed a crowd that was unresponsive – that did not provide psychological visibility for his ego – he terminated his speech quickly and left the scene.

Arrested Development

The normal, psychologically healthy human being is born with a strong desire to learn. As the growing child enters puberty this condition is complexed with an overpowering emergent sexual component that forms this desire into a formidable drive to learn, apply the learning, and create value according to his personal ethical direction. With the emerging student of the intellect, this drive to learn, apply, and accomplish extends, essentially, to the end of his life. Such was *not* the intellectual development of Adolf Hitler.

For one major reason, covered later in this chapter, Hitler's intellectual (and personality) development was stunted, essentially coming to an end at about the age of 16. His fundamental outlook on life was shaped at that age and remained, for the most part, unchanged until his death. This is *not* to say that Hitler, the man, did not learn. It *is* to say that the learning accomplished by Hitler, the man, was always *acutely* limited by early first concepts, and channeled into those intellectual streams that supported basic decisions and opinions already accepted. After his early learning period, the things Adolf Hitler allowed to be incorporated into his mental equipment were things that supported the technical implementation of his fundamental learning. Hitler, the man, had accepted what Adolf, the boy, had placed into the intellectual core of his psyche and that would not change. The introverted nature that supported this mind-set would continue to cripple his ability and willingness to learn new fundamentals, if they had the effect of invalidating or even altering previous important opinions. He, himself, described this intellectual/emotional condition by repeatedly declaring himself to be as, "hard as granite" and as "cold as ice." Such statements were the dedication of his conscious to the unalterable support of his subconscious, locked-in mind-set that had occurred in the socially poorly adapted and terribly frightened and withdrawn teenager of the Vienna years. Such a mentality in the individual set in the average social environment would be considered only an aberration. In the person of a totalitarian dictator of a dynamic and militarily powerful nation state in the center of Europe, it was an enormous and important fault. If the world view of such a politically powerful individual did not comport with reality, the capability for great destruction was established that began to be effected immediately as Adolf Hitler, the Chancellor of Germany, took the political reins of the state apparatus on 30 January 1933.

The National Effect

The German nation and society was in a shambles in 1933 when Hitler assumed the Chancellorship. This condition ranged from the social to the political to the economic. The German public was ready and willing to accept anyone as head of government who promised to improve the living condition and bring safely and order to the streets of German cities, many of which were repeatedly torn and disrupted by violent Communist agitation. After the lack of control and disorder of the early Weimar years, especially in Berlin, people were satisfied to accept a certain amount of regimentation. He could give them that. But his sense of understanding of the desire of the people, generally, to live their lives freely, without interference from any outside and unwelcome source, was absent. His world view of the national condition had been truncated by his adolescent view of Richard Wagner's various operatic motifs and the severe elements of his early upbringing, and his intentions and efforts were concentrated on causing such views to be accepted by the German people. He would not accept the extensive and sophisticated view of human society possessed by the public, and attempted to replace the contemporary German sociology with one of his own – a Wagnerian sociology of Seigfrieds, Wotans, Lohengrins, and Rienzi di Colas all designed and aimed at his own personal institutionalization in the society as the savior of Germany, worshiped by an adoring and compliant public of his own making. Adolf Hitler, the newly enabled German dictator of 1933, viewed the complex and very solidly stratified German society in just the same way as Adolf Hitler the teenaged boy had - he was still an outsider. In spite of his political position and his political power, he still was not accepted by high classed Germans (and especially the nobility) as an equal. The important consequences of this situation were two in number. First, Hitler's desire to be accepted, his craving for psychological visibility was still being denied. Second, his control of the German society was thwarted by the presence of the intellectuals, the nobility, and especially by the self-contained regimentation of the army. In

1934 the program for the virtual complete control of the army was first initiated by the murder of Ernst Rohm and the SA hierarchy and the "Furher Oath" taken by the army, and then consolidated by the subsequent tremendous expansion of the military, as he tore up the Versailles Treaty in 1935. The German civilian society was both encouraged and forced over the middle years of the 1930s by an ever more invasive government program of "social leveling", aimed at bringing the general German society to a condition of the lowest common denominator, which could then be more easily controlled by the Nazi apparatus. The program for the conversion of the German people into one monolithic socialist society based on "blood and soil" was pressed with ever increasing scope by the Nazi government and party. The "folkish" ideal of a handful of German and Austrian malcontents was being institutionalized in the German society, for the purpose of allowing Adolf Hitler, finally, to "belong", become important, and achieve the psychological visibility his stunted psyche had craved since childhood. In the middle 1930s Adolf Hitler finally and truly became the German Fuhrer, both in his own mind and in the overwhelming majority of German citizens.

His initial efforts with this goal met with only partial success (in spite of Goebbels' potent propaganda machine); people had been fooled by politicians before. His success at limiting countervailing opinions about him and his programs was much more efficacious with the establishment of the concentration camps in the spring of 1933, only a couple of months into his administration. This conscious adoption of Lenin's and Stalin's method of social domineering and control would continue to the end, in 1945. His ignorance of the very high intellectual level and sophistication of the German people resulted in a squashing of that society by means of physical force coordinated with a very potent propaganda. His efforts in affecting nation states not under the direct physical control of the Gestapo (while initially extensive) was less successful, over time. With foreign countries and governments, the difference of his ignorant world view with the contemporary facts of reality could not be solved by the use of the Gestapo and concentration camps; this lack of compliance would have to be solved by the German army.

The International Effect

The Germans are a talented and well organized nation state in modern times. When something peaks the interest of one German, there is very quickly a dozen or more looking into the new "find" and recording and systematizing all the correlated information that can be uncovered. They are great "records keepers." Germans are a curious lot, who strongly desire to learn and know new things. They have produced Kants and Hegels, Mozarts and Beethovens, Schillers and Goethes, and Heisenbergs and Einsteins. Even the Iron Chancellor, Otto von Bismarck, was known for his great organizational and administrative capabilities. Adolf Hitler was *not* one of this class of men.

Hitler's arrested development at about age 16 and his lack of good formal education at any level left him abysmally ignorant of contemporary world affairs, for a head of state. The upper level of the Nazi hierarchy (with the possible exceptions of Goring and Speer) were all conforming men of quite limited abilities; *and all of them were "yes men"*, who would willingly subordinate their intellects to his desires. Hitler, himself, had seen to that; he wanted no more contemporary August Kubiceks at this late date to "show up" his lack of artistic or intellectual ability, by contrasting example. It is true that there existed many very smart people in the government bureaucracy, having a very large and complete knowledge of contemporary international events. But these were not people who had access to the only personality that really mattered in the totalitarian dictatorship that was Nazi Germany of the late 1930s.

Hitler did have a certain knowledge of people, but this was of a kind that was able to predict and control direct individual responses to his own initiatives, by means of a crude and overbearing personal attitude. When he considered interactions with a Neville Chamberlain or an Edouard Daladier or a Josef Stalin the interaction was one of a personal one-on-one nature with very little or no consideration of the national/international context represented by these leaders. This is what he expressed when he said about the Munich meeting in September of 1938, "I saw my enemies at Munich. They were little worms." The underlying reason for this "shallowness" of viewpoint was simply a lack of knowledge of the countries and the people represented by these leaders – in short, an ignorant world view. Unlike the Germans, the French and the English did *not* have dictatorial leaders. unlike his own (very sketchy) knowledge of German history, social movements, and folkish philosophy, he had little or no corresponding knowledge of France and especially England. His lack of contextual international knowledge caused him to make decisions and initiate actions, including military actions, that a smarter and more knowledgeable head of state would not have attempted. At first, the consequences of his stupidities were obviated and overcome by a strong desire of the western democracies for "peace at any price" and the overwhelming talent and capability of the German military - *a condition not of his doing.*

Hitler's knowledge of geopolitical history *did* include one very important fact – the knowledge of what a two front war had meant to Germany in WW I. Hitler, himself, had never served on the eastern front during the war, but he (like all Germans) was aware of the frightening effects caused in the Prussian population as the Czar's army hordes advanced toward the very heart of Germany, before they were stopped at Tannenberg by Ludendorf and Hindenburg. He was also aware of the great weakening of the German military if it was required to split its resources between west and east. He remembered the desperation associated with the German effort to somehow get the Russians out of the war by use of the "sealed train" from Switzerland containing V.I. Lenin, and the hope that such a rabble-rouser could cause additional trouble in an already very troubled Czarist political world. Thus, the all-out effort to establish a non-aggression treaty with Josef Stalin's Soviet Union before the attack on Poland commenced. His knowledge of the military/economic capabilities of the USSR in 1939 was only marginally better than his corresponding knowledge of the United States, but he was somewhat familiar with the government apparatus established by Stalin, and Stalin, himself. He greatly admired Josef Stalin and he had borrowed and adapted numerous programs and tactics from the Soviet political apparatus for use in Germany. Hitler authorized Foreign Minister Ribbentrop to make any concessions necessary to secure a pact with Stalin before the scheduled Polish attack of September 1. This was accomplished on 23 August. His eastern border was secure. But the phenomenal diplomatic effort spent by Hitler to secure this treaty of non-aggression in August of 1939, was, incredibly, discarded with careless abandonment only a year and a half later in the early spring of 1941, when the plans for Operation Barbarossa, the all-out attack on the Soviet Union were finalized. After his tremendous victories on the continent in 1940-41, Hitler's attack on England had failed and his world reputation (created by the German military) suffered. His intellectual judgment regarding political and military actions was as limited as ever (he simply would not or psychologically *could not* learn), but his fragile self-esteem desperately required support, still again. Reacting with abysmal ignorance of the facts of political and military reality facing him, the Soviet Union was attacked in June of 1941, on a broad front. This action was nothing less than a replay, on an international scale, of his continuing addiction to the external approval and adoration of his audiences to his endless speech-making of previous years. His military and international political ignorance, and his arrested intellectual development, would not allow him to learn new things, even from the best military leadership the world had ever seen; but his delicate and fragile ego required a continuing and never-ending support to justify his personal reason for existing as a human being. This love and support he now got from a people welded to him by the danger and distress of war.

But to throw a little better clarity into the mind, knowledge, and world view of Adolf Hitler in the quiet European Summer of 1939 through the disastrous month of December 1941, the following is observed.

1. On page 396 of his book, *The Psychopathic God: Adolf Hitler*, Robert Waite says, "Hitler's prewar diplomacy may be seen as a triumph of opportunism and cunning. It can also be seen as a series of invitations to disaster.

   Three different interpretations may be considered. First, in the unlikely event that A. J. P. Taylor is correct in insisting that all Hitler really wanted was peace in his time and a negotiated revision of Versailles, then the methods he employed to attain those ends were "singularly inappropriate." Second, if we are to suppose that Hitler wanted only a limited, localized war with Poland to gain Danzig and the Corridor, his belligerent speeches against Western powers, his atrocities against minority groups, and his broken promises to both British and French statesmen show him proceeding in ways that were unlikely to isolate Poland and most likely to prod his victim's strong allies to come to her defense. Finally, if he really plotted the great European war of conquest he had promised in *Mein Kampf*, in his second book of 1928, and in dozens of public and private speeches, his preparations for fighting such a war were conspicuously inadequate. The scholarly Franz von Halder, chief of the Army General Staff in 1939, said in an interview that "unbelievable as it may sound, he [Hitler] did not even have a general plan for the war."" [The author hastens to point out that such a lack of preparation by Hitler for the war is what one would expect from a limited intellect engaged in "playing-at-war games" as a man, just as he did as a youth. If his intellectual development was strongly arrested at age 16, as proposed, this shortcoming and many that followed may be explained.]

2. In the very next paragraph Waite says, "Hitler also failed to give the orders to supply his army. Halder recorded in his diary that there were monthly shortages of 600,000 tons of steel, and that munitions in general were in such short supply that no large-scale combat was possible. "Supply was sufficient for only one-third of the available divisions for fourteen days. Current production was just enough to keep the same one-third active." "[This failure (and that in numbers 4 and 8 below) is highlighted by his later clumsy attempts to feed his wartime economy by suddenly switching the German army's assault direction from Moscow toward the Ukraine for "economic reasons."]

3. Hitler ordered the German panzer units operating under Heinz Guderian against essentially no resistance, to stop in actual sight of the port of Dunkirk, which allowed most of the British army to be evacuated to England, as an army still "in-being." This was done, ostensibly, to impress the British with his magnanimity and bring

28

them to the negotiating table. Such was the level of his understanding of his most powerful enemy, to that date.

4. Later on the page Waite notes, "Economic mobilization was not really ordered until the autumn of 1944 – that is, well after his 'Fortress Europe' had been entered from the West and Russia was moving in from the East. Only then, when it was much too late, did Hitler move haltingly in the direction of full economic mobilization."

5. On page 397 Waits says, "Almost any historian, serene in the knowledge of how the future turned out, can look back on a lost war and point out the strategic errors which led to defeat. It is also indubitably true that even the most brilliant military commander can make a mistake. But Hitler's blunders were so many, so costly, and so gratuitous as to suggest that these "mistakes" were the result of a strong, unconscious impulse for self-destruction." [The author points out that these "blunders" can also easily be explained by an intellectual dullness, that obviated any new fundamental learning and adaptation by the developmentally arrested dictator.]

6. Hitler ignored the well-documented and well-founded advice of his military intelligence when they told him of the tremendous size and capability of the Russian war-making machine and the quality of their weapons, reported from information gleaned from records and first-hand knowledge from the late 1920s, on.

7. Hitler invaded the Soviet Union much too late in the year in 1941, and then after his forces had been squandered in the Balkans and Greece.

8. Hitler declared war (completely unnecessarily) on the United States on 11 December 1941, right in the middle of the worst defeat of Germans arms to that date in W W II. He did this in spite of observations and recommendations by his most knowledgeable strategic advisors that the potential

of American industry and arms was by far the most threatening and formidable of any nation in the world.

These events, and indeed many others right up to the end in 1945, taken together raise serious questions about the intellectual condition of Adolf Hitler, per se. Historians, psychologists, and even psychiatrists have resorted to various scenarios to explain the man's behavior and render intelligible some of his decisions regarding German foreign policy and military operations, both strategic and tactical. Some have said he was mentally unbalanced – a manic depressive. Some have claimed he had a neurological disease – such as Parkinsonism. Some have blamed everything on Dr. Morell, his physician, for dosing him with various outrageous "remedies", including methamphetamine. Some have claimed he was suffering from advanced syphilis, contracted as a young man in Vienna, and some say he was a victim of "split-brain" pathology. There is even an historian who claims that Adolf Hitler was a victim of political and other external forces he could not control, and that he was actually a "weak dictator." In the author's opinion, this last is patent nonsense. Finally, some (many) writers have simply claimed that Adolf Hitler was a psychopath – perhaps simply delusional or perhaps schizophrenic. After all this is considered, perhaps there is a better and simpler explanation for a life and career that affected so many people in such a horrid manner.

The Underlying Psychological Determinant

The author does not take issue with many or even most of the personal psychological arguments and analyses presented in a huge number of books and papers written about Adolf Hitler. But he does take issue with the claim that any of these are fundamental in nature and capable of standing on their own in the explanation of important and critical events concerning the dictator. The author claims that any or all of the arguments used to explain the consummate evil that was Adolf Hitler can be reasonably and suitably superimposed on a basic condition and psychological essence that composed the human being who became the Fuhrer of the Nazis and the Savior of the German people. That basic condition is not at all complicated, and this was the major *fundamental* reason for his arrested development at about age 16.

The author proposes that Adolf Hitler was, simply, *not a very smart human being*. This is not to say that the man was dimwitted, he was not. A measurement of intellectual capability done in the modern method would not class Hitler as a moron or an idiot, but the author does believe that such a measurement would show the man to be intellectually dull/normal – perhaps with a measured IQ of some 90 points, or so. It is true that Hitler did have "trick memory," with which he could confound some very intelligent people with the idea that he was quite smart; but such eccentricities are familiar, indeed, to psychologists who study the human phenomenon described by the term *idiosavant*, or "wise idiot". These people often can do things that would lead the casual observer to conclude that they possessed a phenomenally high intelligence; but the extraordinary "talent" is confined to a very small range of intellectual operations, and the person, overall, is intellectually dull or even grossly deficient.

It is also true that Hitler limited his inner circle to those who were not very smart or even well-educated. (The author believes that Hitler was completely aware of his own lack of intellectual keenness, and obfuscated that condition strongly to the people surrounding him.) The few exceptions to this rule were those who were totally "taken" with him and his leadership, to the extent of the religious "true believer", which they, indeed, actually were! If anyone else tried to "get too close" to the Fuhrer he confounded them with lies and otherwise misleading statement and actions. He did this specifically and on purpose (in his own words) because he did not want anyone to be able to "know" him (and reveal his intellectual weakness to the world). He read little, had only a grade school education, with which, at that, he was not very successful, and displayed no individual talents *at all*, with the exception of a primitive and comparatively poor capability for drawing.

In their book, *A Brotherhood of Tyrants* Hershman and Lieb say on page 72, "Hitler craved power, but government did not interest him and he refused to learn anything about it. In only two areas did he concern himself with details; foreign policy and the armed forces. Otherwise, as Albert Speer reported, 'he trusted in his inspirations no matter how inherently contradictory they might be ....' Or as the

Fuhrer himself declared, 'One must listen to an inner voice and believe in one's fate.' When it came to governing Germany, Hitler would give vague orders. Others had to work out the means to fulfill them."

In the very next paragraph Hershman and Lieb report, "Historian Oswald Spengler complained: 'He cannot work.' This was an oblique observation by Spengler of Hitler's actual intellectual condition that he *could not change his thinking*, and he had always thought of himself as the *artist dilettante*, doing no "work" but simply playing at (his version of) the artist's life of ease and leisure. Between the middle 1930s and the h eight of WW II, he said many times, to many people that he simply *could not change*. Hitler also refused to face problems. Dr. Hermann Rauschning, president of the Danzig senate observed, 'when difficulties arose, he simply pushed aside everything he had just planned and lost all interest in the pile of wreckage that remained behind.'" This is the typical reaction of a limited intellect to problems too difficult for him to solve or even grasp.

Later on the page it reads, "Hitler said that had the First World War not come about, he would 'probably have become one of the foremost architects, if not the foremost architect of Germany.' But he was not an artist distracted by politics, he was a dictator dilettante. Hitler surrounded himself with artistic failures like himself. Joseph Goebbels, the Minister of Propaganda and Public Enlightenment, was a failed novelist; Alfred Rosenberg, head of the Foreign Political Office of the Nazi party, was an unsuccessful architect. This could include many others in the Nazi political entourage. Hitler applied what he thought were artistic standards to everything, including weapons of war. Generals should also be artistic, Hitler thought. When he began WW II, he was willing that the army draft scientists and technicians and send them to the front, but he exempted the musicians of the Berlin Philharmonic." For a man possessing a normal intellectual acumen this would be insanity. The content of essentially all his writing and especially his speeches from about 1920 on, were generalized platitudes, interjected with statements of extreme hatred for this subject or that, and a virulent Jew-bating. He failed at every single thing he tried, that required some intellectual capacity for success. As a belligerent, loud-mouthed agitator he *was* successful in the field of politics.

His genetic heritage reveals no one on either side of his family tree who could be classed as intellectually astitute - going as far back as the records allow. His family tree on both sides showed the probability of some inbreeding, which often results in individuals of substandard intelligence. The only thing at which he excelled was oratory, and this only because he could not control his emotions (any small amount of anger tended to generate more and deeper anger) and had a loud and raucous voice, which tended to inspire a certain amount of respect in those who appreciate aggressive things as *attractively masculine* in a man and leader. The inability to control one's temper had a loud and (often) scurrilous voice are also often signs of lower than average intelligence, as is a belief in the supernatural, in modern times.

He had been aware, since the Linz days, that displays of temper could often get him what he wanted from other people. He had learned this by example from his father, and the later use of the method on a doting and concerned mother was often successful. This (unfortunate) learning was evidently at least one of the reasons he rarely and almost never made friends. As long as he could approach a relationship as a subordinate (e.g., child to man), he was often successful; such a relationship did not require an intellectual component of any note, but simply agreement and obedience. The same situation existed in his earlier childhood relationships, which were mostly with younger children who could (one would guess) rarely become intellectually threatening. Beyond the early grade school years, which required little mental capability, Adolf was ever less academically successful and more of a problem in deportment. He was learning that emotional responses easily deflected any sort of intellectual criticism, and that shouting down an opponent tended to place him in control of matters – matters at least of an immediate nature. This syndrome, which would stay with him and only grow stronger with the years, would prove to be his most effective method of personal control, as Fuhrer, with state power supporting his tantrums and screaming.

The Twisted Mind-Set

After his mother died, and after he left Vienna for Munich, Hitler was something of a lost soul for several years, with no training, no capabilities, and no talent of any note. WW I came to his rescue in

August of 1914, and the 25 year old (militarily exempted from the draft in Austria due to poor health) enlisted in the Germany army (not the Austrian). Several chance events on the Western front convinced a very superstitious and mystically minded Hitler that he had received the protection of God, and was, thus, destined for great things later in life. This very same thought pattern emerged after the failed bomb plot of 20 July 1944, when the chance relocation of the bomb satchel not only spared his life, but left him with few physical injuries, while some of those around him were killed or gravely injured. He explained this to a visiting Mussolini later that same day as a supernatural determination that Fate was not done with him, in spite of the Normandy invasion and disaster after disaster on the Russian front. He still had great things to accomplish; he would still win the war, after all. The denial of obvious facts of reality is evident, in this attitude.

The post WW I adaptation was quite problematic for Adolf Hitler, as it was for many German ex-soldiers, who simply refused to be discharged into civilian life and create their own destinies, de novo. Political intrigue, riots, and take-overs of whole areas of Germany by Soviet backed Communist groups was instrumental in the creation of "Free Corp" paramilitary gangs determined to replace the Red totalitarian rule with one of their own. They were ex-military, used to living in a dictatorial environment (which all militaries are), and they wanted no part of the Russian "virus."

The ideological part of this movement was present, in abundance, in the beer cellars and meeting halls of Munich, in Bavaria, and was (as a generality) something the still organized and existing Germany army wanted to keep track of. Adolf, the youth, had learned the basics of his oratory skills in Linz and Vienna, and Adolf Hitler, the man, was now honing those skills in the Munich environment. He was now learning that shouting, emotionalism, and belligerence were potent weapons in the arsenal of the orator, who desired to move and control people. He found such behavior especially effective in countering intellectual arguments he could not follow, and opinions and statements with which he disagreed. And he also found, much to his surprise, that such actions attracted a certain percentage of the general public to him as a leader of opinion. He did not need to understand what he talked about, but only shout it loudly and display emotion. Hitler was beginning to achieve notoriety with the German public, and the extreme nationalist groups that thrived in the Munich political environment.

Captain Mayr, German army, became aware of the loud-mouthed agitator and enlisted him to join and spy on one of them, the German Workers' Party, which had had an on-again/off-again existence since the beginning of the century. Hitler continued to use shouting, anger, and emotionalism as a substitute for a lack of intellectual efficacy and quickly rose to a position of leadership in the small political party, destined to become the National Socialist Workers' Party of Germany – the Nazis. The rest, as they say (with numerous twists and turns) is history. but the major single element in that history was Adolf Hitler. National Socialism, what is stood for and what id did, is unthinkable with Adolf Hitler at the helm. The question is, how did Hitler get there and what talents did it require for him to do so?

The Teppischfresser

The author's claim that Adolf Hitler was quite intellectually limited and something of an idiosavant leads to the following observations and conclusions.

1. Hitler's father taught the boy aggressive control of others, belligerence, and temper tantrums by example.

2. Hitler was unsuccessful in any "intellectual" endeavor – his "trick memory" or condition of being an idiosavant, excepted.

3. The typical emotional, belligerent response to being bested at something (chess, bridge, intellectual argument, etc.) is to "turn over the table." This is, overcome opposing intellectuality with personal attacks and/or force. Hitler's ability to exert personal physical force was *very* limited (he was scrawny, pot bellied, short-legged, light-weight, and anatomically poorly built, so that he used surrogates as ruffians and assassins. He, himself, once said, obliquely addressing this shortcoming, "You can fight with your mouth!"

4. Hitler had a very large library but read little beyond his school years. This action is typical of an intellectual "light weight" trying to impress others.

5. Music is an intellectual/emotional art form. Hitler responded almost exclusively to the emotionalism of Wagner and not the intellectuality of Beethoven, Mozart, or Bach.

6. Adolf, the boy, always loved *playing war* with his young schoolmates. Adolf Hitler the military commander enlarged his scope considerably and continued to "play war" through Poland, Western Europe, England, North Africa, and finally Russia. In spite of the claims of some writers, Hitler's military bungling and sometimes outright stupidity bordering on insanity lost W W II for a German military that was head-and-shoulders above any other military in the world. The only comparable power in the 1939-41 period was England, and that only on the seas.

7. During the reorganization of the Nazi Party, after his time in prison, he more and more used the method of displaying personal anger to subordinates and contemporaries alike, and sometimes at the most inappropriate times and in the most irrational manner. All during the war and years and before he used temper tantrums and the most belligerent threats of force to get his way with politicians and even heads of state. At the time this was written off as mere tactics. The author believes these "tactics" were perhaps more likely an accurate description of his actual uncontrolled state of mind – the state of mind of an intellectual incompetent trying to exist and operate in complex situations for which he was not equipped and about which he had little true understanding. The failure to understand that the political positions of France and England had become fixed in August of 1939 (because of his own actions), and that his international temper tantrum by the use of surrogates (the German army) would not be cost-free, was only the first of a series of blunders that he would commit, one after the

other, until the Red army came knocking at the door of the Fuhrer bunker in 1945.

8. During the conduct of the war, Hitler browbeat his generals and admirals with seemingly no care at all of what their training and talents told them were the right military decisions to make. This, in the face of the most resounding feat of arms ever seen in modern times in Poland and Europe, by the most awesome military tactical and strategic operational staffs in history. (The credit given Hitler by some historians for the Ardennes offensive in 1940 is misplaced. This very insightful and successful strategic operation was initiated and planned by Colonel General Friz Erich von Manstein. The general staff was dead set against Manstein's risky plan but Hitler had shown an interest in meddling in strategic military planning ever since the Polish campaign. Manstein (and others of a like mind) agreed to "engineer" the plan with Hitler to get it approved, and to give him credit for it.) Even a very fragile self-esteem in the presence of the military hierarchy (some of whom were royalty) does not explain his irrationality. He simply did not understand or accept that he was still a "little boy" playing at war, in the presence of very talented military professionals who could not tell him to "get lost" because he was Head of State, and because they had been forced to swear an oath of loyalty to him, personally.

9. The author believes that Hitler had been aware of his lack of normal mental competence since the Linz (or Styr) days, and that this knowledge continued to affect his personally abusive frame of mind at an accelerated pace as his political power expanded and his condition became more complicated. This "awareness" was recognized subconsciously, mainly since a full, conscious acceptance would have been too destructive for his very low self-esteem, which became more and more threatened as the years passed. His later uncontrolled temper tantrums

following even the mildest disagreements and his psychological rigidity are prima facie indicators of the fragile nature of his perilously constructed personality – the result of a fear of being observed as intellectually unable to function as Fuhrer.

This "playing at war" by Hitler was not lost on his most talented military who came in contact with him. True, there were the young military cadre of former Hitler Youth and also the SS and former SA bully-boys who had come to believe the Fuhrer to be an essentially, supernatural Savior of Germany. This group did exist in the military establishment, but the early old-line upper echelon commanders had no such supernatural beliefs about Hitler. They simply had to obey him because, and only because, he held the "big stick" of unquestioned command over them, generated in accordance with the German political system they were a part of.

In conversations and meetings with civilians and military Hitler used his temper tantrums and the associated physical actions to squelch argument, convert dissenting opinion, and simply "get his way" about any particular matter. Quite often he seemed to actually lose control of his targeted displays of temper (which were almost always his form of conscious "acting") and become literally *taken over* by the originally self-generated spate of anger to the point of a true loss of control of his mind and body. In these fits of insanity he would actually lie on the floor of the room he was in, froth at the mouth, scream uncontrollably, tear at the carpet, and pound his fists on the floor. This was simply a more extreme form of the mannerisms and actions that he used in hundreds of speeches in beer cellars and meeting halls across Germany, and it earned him the sobriquet of *teppichfresser*, or "carpet chewer." Whether he actually chewed the edges of carpets during these fits cannot be definitely verified by the author, but the fact that the Chancellor and Fuhrer of Germany was the equivalent of a petulant 8 year old boy, with totalitarian power is not arguable. The results of this incredibly irrational and unbelievably destructive combination, made possible by a strongly socialist oriented German state, would be acted out first on the European and then, the world stage between 1938 and 1945.

CHAPTER 4

Creation of the Nazi Religion

Hitler's informal, unofficial "education" in the Vienna years from 1908 to 1913, had two main components – the political and the mystical. The writers and pamphleteers who would turn out to be the most important in the mental development of the introverted teenager strongly propounded both these components, more or less equally. Of this collection of individuals Richard Wagner, Georg Lanz von Liebenfels, Guido von List, Theodor Fritsch, and Gustave Le Bon are probably the most important.

Wagner

The contribution of Richard Wagner to Hitler's adolescent development would be hard to overemphasize. This contribution has been covered in detail by several good modern histories, so the author will not rehash this literature. What he will do is point out and emphasize the effect that Wagner had on Hitler with his political arguments and his Teutonic mysticism, thundering down the closing years of the 19th Century in close step with his enormously emotionally moving music. The effect that Wagner's music has on the classical initiate is hard to explain, because that effect is so fundamentally striking and important. To say that Hitler was captivated by Wagnerian opera would be gross understatement; the political components to Wagnerian philosophy came along for the ride. The old Teutonic myths of Siegfried, the ancient Germanic god Wotan, the more modern epic tales of Rienzi and Tannhauser were all put to music by Wagner in operas, which captured the limited young Adolph in an emotional way that caused him to accept Wagner's extensive philosophical writings without much question, and for the rest of his life. Wagner's antisemitism, his religious orientation against Christianity and for the old Germanic paganism, and his dynamic and captivating musical genius of historic proportions all gained important recognition and adoption into what would become no less than the institutionalized German religion of Naziism, over the short period from the early 1930s through the end of WW II in 1945, and continues to exist in small measure even today.

The Conversion: Artist to Politician

The second failure to gain admission to the Vienna art school was not only a very bitter pill for Adolf to swallow, it contained a strong but subliminal message to his subconscious, which the author believes controlled much of what the individual, Adolf Hitler, said and did. The boy's psyche badly needed a belief in the mystical to justify his ego and self-esteem in the face of the unquestioned rejection by the Viennese society of his conscious artistic abilities. But his mind would simply not relax the belief that he *was* an artist and was well-suited to be an artist. His close relationship with Wagner, the extraordinarily powerful musical artist, brought ever nearer the political side of the Wagner persona – especially as it seemed that he had nowhere else to go. His mother's death and his rejection by Vienna severed any strong ties to his birth country, and his move to Munich opened the way for a gelling of the basics of the philosophies of Wagner, Lanz von Liebenfels, Guido von List and several others in his mind, together with a virulent nationalism that festered in the southern German province of Bavaria.

WW I interrupted the difficult and not very effective intellectual effort Hitler was trying to apply to his status quo in his environment, and his newly discovered *German* nationalism found him enlisting in the German army. The next 4+ years of additional maturity and the personal experience of the horror that is combat, left no doubt in his mind that art was not a vocation at which he would prosper, or even survive. His pre-war learning now came to control the fundamental drive of his thinking, and the philosophy and politics of pan-Germanism, accentuated by the selling-out of Germany by "evil" politicians in 1918, dominated his mind. From now on politics would consume the time and actions of the loud-mouthed agitator, and Wagner, the pan-German and Jew-baiter could contribute his absent effect to the effort.

The political role was, for Hitler, not his first choice as a profession. Politics was, in the European scheme of things a less than elevated calling – not a thing anyone with any "class" at all would care to devote his life to. This would apply especially to an artist. But Hitler had two strong driving forces leading him into politics – he was at a dead end as an artist and his infatuation with German nationalism was becoming more and more important to him. And besides, he had no other talent at all at which he could hope to make a living – even in his own mind. His 1930s musing about being an architect were a latter day dream, which he could voice openly and be seriously considered only because he was dictator at the time. He could plainly see (and appreciate) the favorable attention his political oratory was brining him, and this was, for his gravely wounded self-esteem, as cold water to a thirsty traveler. He could plainly see that the positive response to his speeches was based on emotion above all, and emotion, to him, meant chiefly, Richard Wagner.

Religion and Naziism

His efforts to place ever more emotion into his public communications very naturally drove him in the direction of religious ideas and beliefs, as it did Wagner. And for Germans (including Wagner, Hitler, and the great majority of their average countrymen) the extraordinary and deeply felt mysticism of ancient (pre-Christian) German myth was something familiar, being in-bred in the common culture. To use religious-styled emotionalism in his oratory, Hitler had to bring it "up to date" – to place a large amount of religious ideas and rhetoric into the common parlance of everyday life for his listeners. This, and his ultimate position as party leader, installed a serious and important religious component into the Nazi movement. But this "installation" was not equal up and down the party hierarchy. Hitler's purpose in placing religious styled rhetoric into his speeches and programs was to garner a belief in him as an actual "lord" of the mediaeval type. His personal belief in mysticism was real and profound but it was strictly a one-on-one relationship with the ethereal and the German historical supernatural. The mystical elements he installed

41

in the Nazi system were there for the conversion of others (and especially young people) to his cause and a literal worship of him as a contemporary Savior, come to earth to save the chosen (German) people and western civilization. Such a social undertaking with great numbers of human beings requires an "us against them" mentality, something already very familiar to Adolf Hitler. He had chosen the "us" in the German people as a whole – a worldwide concept. The "them" would become the major socialist world competitor for Naziism, the Communist regime of Josef Stalin, with the inclusion of the Jewish race into the mix as the founders and foremost proponents of Communism in western Europe. This inclusion would be an easy thing for him to do, since Karl Marx was, in fact, a Jew, large numbers of Communists, worldwide, were Jews, and Jews were the single most talented, richest, and most economically and socially aggressive people in Europe. Hitler believed in the veridicality of the, *Protocols of the Elders of Zion*, a 19th Century Russian secret service fabrication (one more indication of his intellectual dullness), so he really believed his pogrom against Jews was justified. In 1943, when it was obvious to all that the war could not be won, the Final Solution was implemented in all areas under Nazi control. If he could not destroy the Communist Jews in Russia, at least he could destroy the Jews in Europe.

The first fundamental requirement of any religion is hero worship; the second is a program of believing, thinking, and living that the membership should or must follow. The three major western religions all follow these requirements. Christianity has Jesus and the *Bible*; Judaism has Abraham (or Moses) and the *Torah*; Islam has Mohammed and the *Koran*; and Naziism has Hitler and *Mein Kampf.* Hitler would not compete, initially or directly, with these three major systems of supernatural belief, but he could form his own synthesis, and he did. In bringing ancient German mysticism to life in his own time, Hitler had "go-by" created for him in the stories and heroism of Richard Wagner's operas and his philosophical writings. He chose to learn from the example. In the take-over of the newly named National Socialist German Workers' Party between 1920 and 1923, he began to install himself into the position of (future) hero; he did this with his rhetoric, his loud mouth, and his ability to convince fellow party members that he was irreplaceable to the party. With the generation of a *party program* he was less successful, because of his own limited intellectual ability, which was made manifest as an inability to think about theoretical ideas not containing a direct political weapon he could use in his speeches and propaganda, and because there were some smart and well-informed people then existing in the party leadership who had their own ideas about party programs.

The development of early Naziism, from February 1920 until Hitler's takeover of German national politics in 1933, was one of an ever further installation of Adolf Hitler into the party movement as Messiah. The development of the party *program* from 1920 to the 1923 putsch was less extensive and much more open to variation. Nevertheless, on 24 February 1920, in the large meeting hall of the Hofbrauhaus in Munich, Hitler spoke and presented the now famous "Twenty-Five Points" – a written outline of what National Socialism was supposed to be – written by Anton Drexler. Hitler, himself, was incapable of articulating a party program beyond generalities and platitudes, and as head of party recruitment and propaganda he was in a position to block proposals by others in the leadership that tended to minimize his own special place in the movement. Hitler was out for political power, and that alone; he had no ability to make a tight, rational argument and cared very little for those who did. He was a cultural philistine by any measure, often displayed shocking public behavior with seemingly Neanderthal views, and disgustingly servile with people of importance. But in March of 1920, Hitler met Dietrich Eckart, who was able to smooth over a little of his crudeness and introduced him to social circles he would have had no possibility of entering, otherwise. He also schooled the young agitator in his own version of anti-Semitic philosophy and provided extensive guidance and solidity to Hitler's development of his personal beliefs and political attitude. Eckhart's effect on Hitler (and Hitler's great respect) was second only to Richard Wagner, and would last to his very end. A strong and continuous battle for the soul of the new National Socialist party was being fought, and the winner would end up holding the reins of the party apparatus. What would he do with those reins?

The early beginnings of Naziism as a religious movement would expand tremendously from 1920 until about 1941, or so. The SA (Sturmabteilung) was formed immediately in August of 1921, after Hitler took over operational control of the party. He had things in mind, following his natural way of thinking, that would require the use of physical force to accomplish. From the beginning the brown shirted SA was patterned after similar organizations in the German Communist movement, who were not bashful about terror and killing to promote their goal of political take-over. The SA were also used as Hitler's first bodyguard unit and would be trained as a front line force to promote the idea of Hitler's goal of becoming the "Savior" of Germany. As the National Socialist organization expanded (largely to Adolf Hitler's oratorical skills), the expansion of the SA and the creation of other National Socialist programs were established as the treasury permitted. There is nothing like bad times to expand the influence and social power of a demagogue preaching "change" and "new ideas," as the American presidential political campaign of 2008 can bear witness. The run-away inflation of 1922-23 was instrumental in expanding the numbers and power of the National Socialist base and Adolf Hitler. It was said, "If you don't have a shirt on your back, you can always put on a brown shirt!"

The social programs of the Nazis went a long way, in the minds of the general public, in placing the social-reorganizing goals of National Socialism in good stead, and the claims of its Fuhrer to be Germany's savior as believable. The abject failure of the 1923 putsch in Munich, and the subsequent incarceration in Landsberg prison, was only a stumbling block in Hitler's rise as Messiah to the German people, and the relative peace and good times of the middle and late 1920s only a delay. The world-wide depression of the early 1930s would be the spring-board for a crude, dull-witted, and ill-mannered Bavarian dolt to be appointed as COO of the German government on 30 January 1933, and achieve a position of political power from which he could actually effect the condition of himself as the German Messiah and national religious icon.

CHAPTER 5

Nazi Mind Conditioning

The extraordinary level of mind conditioning practiced by the NAZI organization on its membership had its origins in the early 1920s in Hitler's attitude about the requirements that must be placed on the Nazi party member. These requirements had their philosophical basis in German Romanticism, something with which every 20th Century German student had been thoroughly saturated, by the state school system. In his book, *The Ominous Parallels*, in Chapter 3 Leonard Peikoff says, "A well-known German historian has remarked that the romanticist element in German thought would appear to Western eyes as *'a queer mixture of mysticism and brutality.'* The formulation errs only in the adjective 'queer.' The mixture's two ingredients have a magnetic affinity for each other: the first makes possible and leads to the second (and not only in Germany)." This philosophical system, having its roots deep in German historical tradition and maturing in the last 19th Century, leads directly to the Hitler phenomenon. Peikoff says, still in Chapter 3, "The concept of faith does not pertain to the content of a man's ideas, but to the method by which they are to be accepted. 'Faith' designates blind acceptance of a certain ideational content, acceptance induced by feeling in the absence of evidence or proof. It is obvious, therefore, why Nazi (and Fascist) leaders insist on faith from their followers. 'Faith writes Hitler,

> is harder to shake than knowledge, love succumbs less to change than respect, hate is more enduring than aversion, and the impetus to the mightest upheavals on this earth has at all times consisted less in a scientific knowledge dominating the masses than in a fanaticism which inspired them and sometimes in a hysteria which drove them forward."

Still later in the chapter Peikoff observes, "Dogma, whether Nazi or otherwise, requires an authority able to give it the stamp of an official imprimature. The Nazi authority is obvious. 'Just as the Roman Catholic considers the Pope infallible in all matters concerning religion and morals,' writes Goering,

so do we National Socialists believe with the same inner conviction that for us the Leader is in all political and other maters concerning the national and social interests of the people simply infallible. [Hitler's authority derives from] something mystical, inexpressible, almost incomprehensible which this unique man possesses, and he who cannot feel it instinctively will not be able to grasp it at all.'"

This is followed by,

Given their commitment to the method of faith (and their tendency to imitate the Catholic Church), it is not astonishing that some Nazis went all the way in this issue. A tendency never given the status of official ideology yet fully prominent in the movement was voiced in a demand made by several of its leading figures (though Hitler himself regarded it as impractical until the Nazis had won the war): the demand that Nazism itself be turned into a full-fledged religion. These voices urged a state religion supplanting the older creeds, with its own symbols, its own rituals, and its own zealots avid to convert Christians into fanatic Hitler-believers, as, once, ancient missionaries had converted pagans into fanatic Christians. "Adolf Hitler," exclaimed one such believer (the Nazi Minister for Church Affairs), "is the truly Holy Ghost!"

Since the time in 1920, when Hitler actually took personal control of the party machinery, his efforts at centralizing political power in himself had been channeled into the training and indoctrination of a cadre of men who held the person of Hitler, himself, as the beginning and end of all things of importance in their lives. The fact that the German people were not ready for and did not want the political system he was erecting, was slowly and surely twisted and bent around to a condition of partial, if begrudged, agreement during the late 1920s by the dedication and the efficiency of the Hitler cadre. This was helped along greatly by a crushing depression brought about by a run-away inflation in 1922-23 that destroyed whole classes of people. WW I reparation payments (especially to France) and the French occupation of the Ruhr contributed mightily to the German economic collapse and fueled a hatred among the German people for everything French, and most things Western. But the hard-over dedication by the people to Adolph Hitler and his Naziism would not come about until the social brainwashing period of the 1930s had taken place on a national scale, topped off by the astounding German victories over their old rivals and conquerors in 1939 and 1940. From the summer of 1940 on, until the Red Army was knocking at the eastern gate of Berlin in 1945, the average man-on-the-street in Germany looked up to and trusted Hitler to the point of worship. Truly, Adolph Hitler was, *for a short while*, the Savior of at least a large part of the German people.

Beer Cellar Psychology

Adolf Hitler was a crude and uncultured man, a condition that existed until his death in 1945. The philosophical knowledge he did possess drifted into his mind in the beer cellars and coffee shops of Vienna and Munich, and from popularized pamphlets written by self-styled Austrian intellectuals (usually of an anti-Semitic nature) and the philosophical musings of Richard Wagner.

The boy, Adolf Hitler, was a poor student and quit school early – a tacet admission of failure. If Adolf Hitler, the man, could be said to be a student of anything, it was of personal power over other people. The reasons for this are covered in detail elsewhere in this work, but the method he chose to implement his desires was one which he observed had such overwhelming power over the minds of men, that they would willingly and gladly sacrifice their lives at his whim. That method was religion, or to be more precise, the mechanisms of the process of "thought control" that all religions use to acquire the extreme dedication and personal sacrifice of their recruits. This is observed in modern times in the more primitive peoples of the earth, where the large and well-policed religion of Islam exists in force. It is also observed on a smaller scale in the mini-religions, existing around the world and especially in the United States, which are often called "cults" by those of the larger and more organize religious groups which have gained acceptance by the general public. The fact that the "accepted" religions differ philosophically little, if at all, from the viscerally despised "cults" is evaded in the thinking of modern, above-board, religious oriented social commentary.

Obviously, Hitler could not design his "system" for the gaining of personal political power as some warmed-over version of an existing religious organization. The close parallels with the existing religion would be a distraction, and the spokesmen of the existing religion would contest his efforts at every step. His system would not be a "new Catholicism" or a "New Lutheranism" but something *really* new – that is, something really new that actually consisted of something very old mixed with a hodgepodge of cheap and shallow ideas gleaned from beer cellar conversations, all folded together into a social program that used the standard modern religious methods of organization and mind-control aimed at unlimited obedience from its recruits. Hitler would take an old, tried-and-true religious methodology and apply that to a mixture of Germanic hero myth and the extreme emotionalism of Wagnerian music to establish his "program for the elevation of Adolf Hitler." The author believes that this "program" drifted into Hitler's mind over a period of years, after WW I, and continuing to gain structure and force as the slowness of his integrative thought processes allowed. His observation that the method of religious indoctrination that he had learned from the Catholic Church as a boy was an extraordinary power, and a power that extended also to grown men, caused him to incorporate these ideas and methods into his own thoughts, speeches, and conversations as soon as he was cognitively able to do so.

To begin with the goal of this process was the expansion and strengthening of the NAZI party, with the war hero, General Erich Ludendorff, in the lead. This changed, completely, at his trial for treason, after the 1923 putsch, when he successfully upstaged Ludendorff (who was also on trial) and assumed the party leadership for once and for all. The vehicle he would use to implement his program in the German people would be the Nazi party, and his methodology would start (and this is of extreme importance to the efficacy of the later Nazi movement) with the young – both boys and girls, desperately looking for something to believe in and work for. After all, they are the easiest to convince and convert.

A strong Nazi party would give his program the social and financial push required for success, and the addition of the SA "bully boys" to the mix would help to convince any fence sitters. Under Hitler's direct supervision, implementation of the program and mind-conditioning German youth to dependence upon and adherence to a thoroughgoing belief in the conversion of the nation state of Germany into a hard-over socialist state that specifically and intentionally socialized people, themselves (not just economic systems) was made. Hitler, himself, was the major driving force behind this novel version of the "new Soviet man", so strongly forced on the Russian people by Lenin and Stalin, the NKVD, the KGB, the GRU, and the Soviet Gulag. In Chapter 12 of his book, Peikoff has Hitler saying to Hermann Rauschning, Nazi President of the Danzig Senate in 1933-34;

> There will be no license, no free space, in which the individual belongs to himself. This is Socialism – not such trifles as the private possession of the means of production. Of what importance is that if I range men firmly within a discipline they cannot escape? Let them then own land or factories as much as they please. The decisive factor is that the State, through the party, is supreme over them, regardless whether they are owners or workers. All that, you see, is unessential. Our Socialism goes far deeper .... [as does the socialism in the United States of 2009.]

> [T]he people about us are unaware of what is really happening to them. They gaze fascinated at one or two familiar superficialities, such as possessions and income and rank and other outworn conceptions. As long as these are kept intact, they are quite satisfied. But in the meantime they have entered a new relation; a powerful social force has caught them up. They themselves are changed. What are ownership and income to that? Why need we trouble to socialize banks and factories? We socialize human beings.

When one considers the modern United States and the two major political parties that have a monopoly on things political (and economic) in the society, one must scratch his head a long time to discern the difference between the modern American political system and that of Hitler's National Socialism of the 1930s. But the German version of socialization, unlike the Russian, would convert individualist oriented Germans by the use of a religion-based methodology of mind-control, which Stalin and the Russian Communist party did not have. Stalin had the political bludgeons of the GRU and the KGB. But Hitler had the SA *and* the Nazi religion to use on the public, later to merge and evolve into a dedicated religious activity group (mimicking the Catholic Inquisition) known as the SS.

In its effort at the socialization of its containing society Hitler won hands down. From 1933 on, until the disasters of WW II began to dismember its believability in 1943, Hitler's program of ensconcing himself as Savior of the German people and sole leader of the Nazi religion grew in intensity and scope. By 1940, Hitler had more dedication to his person by Germans as the German savior than the Pope did as the leader of German Catholicism. He was finally the hero his stunted and twisted self esteem had always craved. The brutalized young boy who matured into the many-times rejected teenager had finally received social absolution – he was important, *he was accepted.*

CHAPTER 6

The Neanderthal Component

Adolph Hitler! Neanderthan!? Mass Murderer! Caveman!? Naziism! Paleo-anthropolgoy!?

What possible connection could there be between a 20th Century politician, the leader of the Nazis, a self-admitted artist, a worshiper of Wagnerian opera and an extinct species of early Man which disappeared about 30,000 years before the present (YBP)? That connection will be made in this chapter; but in order to do so, a brief diversion must be made into anthropology as applied to the human condition on the earth ranging between the present and some 14 million YBP.

In making that connection, the author will introduce the reader to so me of the literary works of the writer, Stan Gooch, who wrote books entitled *Total Man* and *The Neanderthal Question* (TNQ). Gooch's central arguments, while not yet generally accepted by paleo-anthropologists, appear to the author to be well-founded. From these ideas this author will make a strong if circumstantial case for a major part of Hitler's genealogy being traceable to Neanderthal origins, which in turn may help to provide explanations for some of the extraordinary things the man said and did.

Modern Man: The Unstable Hybrid

The fact that Neanderthal was a viable and quite successful form of early Man is unquestioned. The fact that Neanderthal Man was eclipsed by Cro-Magnon Man in Europe, and elsewhere some 30,000 to 10,000 YBP is also unquestioned. Exactly how and exactly when this happened is a little more open to speculation.

In his book, The Neanderthal Question, Gooch places the very similar simian ancestors of Neanderthal and Cro-Magnon (Kenyapithecus and Ramapithecus) in Africa and northern India some 14 million and 12 million YBP, respectively. He argues that proto Cro-Magnon became trapped in a region of northern India as a group, finally, by the series of Pleistocene glaciation events, while proto Neanderthal was able to retreat south into the more tropical areas in Africa (and the Far East). His arguments for the considerable species physiological/anthropological differentiation between Cro-Magnon (a 6 foot, white skinned, erect, blue-eyed race) and Neanderthal (a 4 ½ or 5 foot, dark skinned, stooped, brown-eyed race) are based on climate, geography, and related conditions, and seem basically quite solid.

Gooch argues that Cro-Magnon, as a group, left its northern Indian origins and first encountered Neanderthal in the Middle East, in modern Israel, where a considerable amount of inbreeding occurred. Mixed breed skeletal remains of some 35,000 YBP support this conclusion. He further extrapolates that all modern men are Neanderthal/Cro-Magnon hybrids, with a great deal of variability of genetic composition from race to race, group to group, area to area, and even individual to individual. He further claims that the hybrid that is modern Man is an unstable hybrid, tending to separate and return to its original components over the years, with this condition superimposed on its normal evolutionary drive – generation to generation.

Gooch's *psychological* arguments regarding Man, the hybrid, are both intriguing and seem to carry some weight, but are more open to interpretation and speculation. However, the anatomical evidence presented in TNQ is based on hard observational evidence. Of course interpretation of even hard evidence must be made, but the core of Gooch's argument for modern Man being a hybrid seems solid.

In spite of the tremendous amount of mixing of the Neanderthal/Cro-Magnon genetics over the last (proposed) 30,000 years, Gooch claims that the Neanderthal and Cro-Magnon anatomical elements can be isolated and observed in modern men the world over. He further claims that the associated psychological characteristics can be isolated and observed, but that both these sets of observations appear as an average set of elements of each genetic grouping that are well mixed in the individual, who may exhibit numerous elements of either type. The author will make use of the Neanderthal descriptor in the following fashion. The term, Neanderthal, will be used to describe a being that lived prior to the proposed interbreeding with Cro-Magnon some 35,000 YBP. The term, "Neanderthal" (in quotes), is used to describe the Neanderthal characteristics of a cross-breed of Neanderthal/Cro-Magnon, and the term, Classical Neanderthal, will refer to pure Neanderthal, further evolved by survival in extreme climate conditions, such as up on the ice sheet of the Wurmian glaciation. Categorizing an individual as either predominately "Neanderthal" or Cro-Magnon is using statistical information that is normally applicable only to groups of people, so that a rational determination of such predominance would require the identification of a meaningful number of one type of characteristic (anatomical and/or psychological) over the other. This is what the author proposes to do in the case of Adolph Hitler.

The Neanderthal Anatomy

The anthropological historian, W.E. Le Gros Clark describes the "pure" form of Neanderthal as having a forward stoop, having short and bowed legs, a curved back ending in a stout neck with large neck muscles. In TNQ Gooch quotes Le Gros Clark as saying,

> The skull differs from modern human skulls in the enormous development of the brow ridges, the receding forehead and the flatness of the skull roof. In all these characters it has a distinctly simian appearance . . . the jaws are massive, the nose unusually broad and the orbits [eye sockets] very large.

> The skull as a whole is of large size, with thick cranial walls. The brow ridges are relatively large, forming a massive shelf of bone overlapping the orbits; the forehead is markedly retreating, the brain case is flattened in a characteristic fashion; the long ridges on the occipital bone [the rear of the skull] are powerfully developed for the attachment of exceptionally strong neck muscles; the occipital region of the skull projects backwards in an angular contour; the orbits

and nasal aperture are large . . . the axis of the *foramen magnum* [the point where the spinal column enters the skull] on the base of the skull is more deflected from the vertical than in *homo sapiens*, suggesting a forward tilt of the head on top of the spine . . . the teeth are relatively large, and the molars in some cases tend to have unusually large pulp cavities combined with fusion of the roots, a condition called taurodontism [or bull teeth – see p., 86] . . . the spinous processes of the neck vertebrae are unusually long for the attachment of the powerful neck muscles.

Adolph Hitler was born in a part of Europe which pre Cro-Magnon Neanderthal occupied heavily, before and perhaps during the Wurmian glaciation. The genetic mixing of Neanderthal and Cro-Magnon arguably occurred later than, and possibly to a smaller extent than, that which is supposed to have occurred about 35,000 YBP in the Middle East. In addition, this area is one in which considerable in-breeding has occurred in more modern times – a process that tends to increase the rate at which an unstable hybrid dissociates. Although it cannot be made definitive, it appears that at least some amount of familial in-breeding occurred on both the paternal and especially the maternal sides of Hitler's genetic tree.

In the third appendix of TNQ, Gooch lists a series of anatomical/psychological characteristics to which he ascribes Neanderthal or Cro-Magnon heritage. He states.

The attributes of our two parental species Neanderthal and Cro-Magnon are mingled in all present-day populations (and in all individuals) of the world. These attributes have of course themselves evolved further in the course of time. *They are not identical in form with the attributes once possessed by our distant ancestors.* **But we can still identify them and see whence they have come.** [Italics and boldface by the author]

In making a case for predicting observed characteristics in modern men as possible or probable, he further states, "'Neanderthal' attributes correlate with each other, as do Cro-Magnon attributes. That is to say, anyone possessing a given Neanderthal quality will *tend* to have others also; but he or she *need* not have others. .... We are speaking, in the following list, always of the *average* values of large groups."

Following this statement Gooch lists 22 attributes in Appendix III of TNQ, to which he assigns pro and anti Neanderthal or Cro-Magnon characteristics. Of this listing the author considers the following 12 as of importance of the identification in this writing. Namely,

NEANDERTHAL	CRO-MAGNON
1. Pyknic body type	Athletic/asthenic body type
2. Short stature	Tall stature
3. Broad, short face	Long, narrow face
4. Round jaw	Square jaw
5. Large ears, eyes, mouth, etc.	Regular features
6. Bushy eyebrows	Thin eyebrows
7. Dark hair	Fair hair
8. Brown eyes	Blue eyes
9. Large cerebellum	Small cerebellum
10. Sloping forehead	Straight forehead
11. Extended occiput	Flat occiput
12. Heavy brow ridges	No brow ridges

In addition to these characteristics the author notes that Gooch treats the case of heavy brow ridges in a special manner on pages 9 and 85 of TNQ. Gooch says on page 9 of TNQ, "Perhaps I can anticipate later discussion by proposing, as already in my earlier books, that the prominent brow ridges of Rhodesian man and *all* Neanderthaloids – occasionally forming a solid shelf, but more often divided by a dip above the nose into two jutting prominences – are the actual, physical model of the horns of the Christian devil." Both Hitler, and several of his inner circle, and especially Deputy Fuhrer Hess, displayed *very* large brow ridges, as well as an extended occiput and faces broader at ear level than at the level of the temples. These characteristics can still be viewed, specifically, in motion picture films taken in the 1930s and 1940s.

Of the 12 listed "Neanderthal" characteristics, one can observe and confirm that, excepting numbers 3 and 9, Adolph Hitler has every single item to a large degree. Hitler's face *was* broad, but not exceptionally so, and a large cerebellum must be inferred from the presence of an extended occiput, since we do not have the results of an autopsy. The pyknic body type, the sloping forehead, the heavy brow ridges, and the extended occiput *all* stand out markedly in several films made during the Nazi era.

Another thing that stands out that is *not* listed in Gooch's Appendix III, is the "waddle" effect he describes in Chapter 9, "The Jews As Neanderthal", page 127. This whole chapter is dedicated to Gooch's belief that Jews, even modern Jews, have over the years maintained more of the Neanderthal element in their genetic makeup than the "normal" westerner. The arguments he makes in this chapter of the book are extensive and credible. He relates about a game played by himself and a Jewish school-friend (Gooch is, himself, Jewish) called "spot the Jew". Among a number of physical characteristics listed for the physical identification of a Jew from a distance, he mentions a characteristic waddle, that he traces to what is universally believed to be a characteristic of the Neanderthal walking gait. Neanderthal was certainly short and stooped over, and the bones of his legs and spine guarantee a waddling sort of walking motion, that Gooch observes is characteristic of the average Jew. Since Gooch makes a strong case for the retention of many Neanderthal anatomical characteristics in a Jewish population that has, more or less, kept itself sequestered over the millennia, the marked waddle displayed by Hitler in many films of the Nazi era may be a further indication of latent Neanderthal anatomical qualities. [It should be pointed out by the author that it has been suggested that Hitler had Jewish ancestry on his father's side, and this characteristic would tend to support that thesis. At best this would indicate a possibility. It is also just as possible that the anatomical trait had no connection at all to any determination of Jewish blood, per se, in his family tree, but was a result of the general set of Neanderthal characteristics in *any* of his ancestors.]

The Neanderthal Mentality

Of the range of mental or psychological attributes that Gooch proposes for Neanderthal, the most outstanding are emotionalism and religion. These characteristics are ascribed by Gooch (and others) to the activity of the cerebellum. On page 109 of TNQ Gooch relates the story of an individual named, Kaspar Hauser.

In 1928 a youth was found standing in the central square of the town of Nuremberg in Germany. He was able to speak barely a few words and had a totally bizarre manner. In his hand he held a note, apparently written by a semi-literate, to the effect that the writer of the note had reared the boy as a foster parent, after the baby had been delivered into his hands in 1812. The writer commended the now youth to the care of the authorities.

Taken into care by a wealthy educationist, Kasper eventually learned to speak and write. His sayings and doings had an apparent quality of mysticism or religious vision – though perhaps some of that was only a childishness of intellect. His own account of his upbringing was that he had been reared in total darkness and had had no contact at all with human beings. Both these statements must be untrue. We know that the eyes do not develop normally unless they are exposed to full, patterned light in the early years. We also know that a plastic period for language learning exists, again in the very early years. If no advantage is taken of the plastic period, the chances of the person learning to speak in later life are virtually, though perhaps not absolutely, nil. What seems certain is that Kaspar had been reared in conditions of severe social isolation and treated from many points of view as might be an unvalued farm animal.

The relevance of this account is that after Kaspar's death the post-mortem revealed an abnormally large cerebellum. Also revealed poor development of the left hemisphere of the cerebrum. The left cerebral hemisphere is normally the dominant one in the majority of individuals and usually houses the main speech centers.

....

Interest centers then on the abnormally large cerebellum. Was this present from birth, a congenital defect (?), which, with the allied cerebral impairment produce a baby what would instantly be recognized, and therefore rejected, as odd? Or

57

did the enlargement of the cerebellum occur as a result either of the impaired cerebrum *or in the gross absence of conscious stimulation such as normally primes the development of the cerebrum?*

The self-isolation of religious mystics is historically well known and extends even to the present around the world and in all cultures. On page 110 Gooch relates.

In 1971 excavation on the site of Norton Priory [in Britain] revealed the skeletons of eighty-five people, most of them monks. Some of the skeletons were perfectly preserved by reason of interment in stone coffins. The remains date from the twelfth century AD.

The remarkable fact that the skulls is that *fifth of the eighty-five show a sizable bulge at the back of the head* – the 'occipital rose' of Neanderthal. Such skull formation, in the general western population today, appears to be only one in every five thousand.

Intelligence, in and of itself, is a difficult term to define, quantify, or even describe in an accurate manner in the general human population. The author believes this to be so because modern Man, the only type of human being whose intelligence has been measured by means of standardized tests, is a hybrid of two species of Man, Neanderthal and Cro-Magnon, whose anatomical intellectual centers, and thus their quality of intelligence, were quite different in the pre-hybrid or "pure" state. According to the Gooch hypothesis the intelligence center of Neanderthal was relatively biased toward the cerebellum, and that of Cro-Magnon was relatively biased toward the cerebrum. Of course the *major* intelligence center of both species was the forebrain, or cerebrum, in which the process of reason is based. The author believes that Adolph Hitler would not have done well on a modern IQ test, which strongly emphasizes the operations of the cerebrum. This does not alter the fact that he possessed some unusual intellectual characteristics, such as a so called "trick" memory. Hitler could and did memorize reams of seemingly unconnected data, especially concerning military topics, which he could then regurgitate, on demand, to confound the arguments of some very intelligent men, such as many or most of his generals in the 1930s and 1940s. This phenomenology (idiosavantism) is well known to modern psychology, and is, if unusual, certainly not extremely rare. (Is this, itself, a Neanderthal characteristic?)

The Religious Elements

Gooch has made it a major thesis in TNQ and other writings that the mentality of the cerebellum is strongly associated with the mystical and the religious, and that of the cerebrum association with the rational and the provable. Adolph Hitler was an *extremely* religious and mystical person, even though he claimed no religious affiliation, except a very early Catholicism from his mother's influence. He was superstitious in the extreme, demonstrating this many times and in many ways, and actually created, de novo, a whole new religion of his own, utilizing elements of Catholicism, ancient Germanic myth religion, Judaism, central Asian religious cults, ancient Egyptian pharaoh worship, and the organized incorporation of his own person into the whole mishmash as the leader of the religion and the actual Savior of the western world. The practical actualization of his religious and mystical thinking was achieved in the SS which, as the 1930s wore on, became institutionalized in the regime as the center point of the Nazi system of belief in state, folk, and Fuhrer. The SS, in their camps, their schools, and their education centers, was Hitler's *Society of Jesus*, and said to be so by Hitler, himself. It is claimed by the author and it seems to be a given from examination of the historical evidence, that Adolf Hitler could never have come even close to achieving the Chancellorship of Germany on the basis o his intellectual, administrative, or interpersonal political talents of rational persuasion. The man was just *far* too limited. He needed the use of the power that religious and mystical beliefs held over men; such was required, and he sensed it.

The author believes this is plainly traced to the fact that Hitler possessed a strong "Neanderthal" component in his genetics, and its exhibition became more and more evident as his political power became more and more enabling. The final result of this cavalcade was a series of decisions and actions tied strongly to his *instinctive* mental processes, without reference to the facts around him and sometimes in stark contradiction to those facts. The results were disasters on a national and world scale, and a retreat by Hitler more and more into a mystical fantasy world in the 1940s, in which Stalingrad could be visualized as a victory and Roosevelt's death in 1945, a deliverance.

CHAPTER 7

The Nazi Religion: Institutionalization

The actual institutionalization of the Nazi religion in Germany was done piecemeal, over the period from about 1922 through the middle of the Russian phase of the war, in about 1943. Prior to 1922 Hitler's influence in German culture was very small, and after the middle of 1943 his cultural influence had evaporated under the disasters of WW II and the terror of the dictatorship. After the resounding defeat at Kursk in July of 1943 and the incessant and highly destructive air attacks from the allied bomber force, the only Germans that continued to have "faith" in Hitler and the Nazi Party were those without choice (the great majority) and the *true believers*.

In the early and mid 1920s Hitler's effect on the society resided mainly in the training of the Nazi cadre (especially after the putsch of 1923) and the ever growing numbers of fellow travelers the movement was attracting. The extraordinarily destructive effects of the runaway inflation of 1922-23 were lasting and still very much operative in the latter 1920s, and more and more of the lower and middle classes succumbed to a shallow-level conversion to Nazi beliefs. This level of conversion would have been much larger, but for two facts. First, Hitler insisted that the party membership be limited to the dedicated, doubtless for the purposes of control; and second, Hitler's Nazi religious practices were in no way fixed and immutable. Hitler wanted true believers that believed in Adolph Hitler, not intellectual understanding by those dedicated to a written creed or a set of fixed ideas. This religion (Hitler's religion) was going to be different from that of the Jews or that of any modern "fixed" religion, Christianity included. Hitler wanted political power over people of the type

Robespierre and Napoleon Bonaparte had, but he wanted more than that. He wanted an emotional power akin to the type possessed by Louis XIV, but much more so, more organized, and more effective. And to accomplish this, his power had to be based not only on politics, and terror, but ultimately, on a deep belief by the people of Germany in the person and personage of Adolph Hitler, himself, - a belief in a complete and mystical sense, of the Christian type, that over a period of some 2,000 years had caused human beings to allow themselves to be tortured and killed in the most horrible ways rather than deny the hero and the essence of their religion, Jesus Christ.

He had observed the great difficulty the Catholic Church and Joseph Stalin were having restricting their ideas and actions to things well-defined and changeless, according to fixed principles, so he followed Mussolini's example in the matter – "Fascism has no armory of theoretical doctrines. Every system is a mistake and every theory a prison." The Nazi religion was engineered as a return to the early conditions of the Christian (and the Soviet Marxist) religion, before the literature and dogma so limited the actions of the leaders. In this way the religion's converts would become extremely faithful to the person of Adolf Hitler (and his disciples), and the religion's leadership could remain unlimited in their desires and their actions./ But to achieve a "religious" faithfulness in its converts, Naziism must have a Savior of the people – just as Christianity had in Jesus Christ – just as Soviet Communism had in Karl Marx. Adolph Hitler would become that Savior of the German people, promoted himself to that position, and required the Nazi propaganda to reinforce this idea – a task so successfully accomplished by that master of propaganda and hard-over *true believer*, Joseph Goebbels.

This program of faith and deification received a large boost in the onset of depression in German (and the rest of the world) in 1930, when desperate people, still suffering from the delayed effects of the 1923 inflation, suffered even more under a grinding depression that affected the entire Western world. There would be no financial help from America, now.

Hitler's program received a critical and *enabling* boost when he was finally appointed as the German Chancellor in January of 1933, by a befuddled old Paul von Hindenburg, lacking even his previous limited level of political discernment. Now for the Fuhrer and Reichschancellor, there existed only one remaining impediment to becoming the Fuhrer and Savior of Germany and taking his place as the "God" of the German people – as Hirohito was in Japan and as Stalin was in Russia – the person of Paul von Hindenburg, himself. Preparations for Hitler taking his unlimited "devine" role in Germany were well underway long before old Hindenburg finally cooperated one final time with Hitler's ambitions, with his death the following year on 2 August 1934. Only two days later Hitler had secured a binding oath of loyalty from all important government personnel and the entire German military, not to Germany or the German Constitution or Republic, but to the person of Adolf Hitler, himself. Hitler now possessed unlimited political power as the German dictator (he had eliminated the annoying political threat of SA leader, Ernst Rohm, in June of 1934) and he would now convert the German people to accepting him as the German Savior by means of propaganda and terror. In the end, only one thing would now dethrone Hitler as Germany's Savior – physical destruction.

Adolph Hitler: Savior

By the end of 1940 Adolph Hitler had taken his place in the large part of the German society as the "ultimate" leader in the religious sense of the term, and with the rest of the people as a world figure without peer. The strong attention the reorganized Nazi party paid to German youth in the late 1920s was beginning to bear fruit by the middle of the 1930s, and even the older, more culturally aware German was being convinced by Goebbels''s very busy propaganda machine, and the very real effects of the development of the country's infrastructure and the military. The Hitler program of deification in the minds of the German youth was very successful, and any potential resistance from older, more aware Germans was being marginalized by Hitler's remarkable success in European politics and Germany's reemergence in European and world affairs. This was strongly supported by Hitler being chosen as *Time's* "Man of the Year" for 1938, and having his photograph placed on the cover of the magazine. If Hitler was viewed as a religious-styled savior by German youth by 1940, he was also viewed as a world-class politician by essentially the rest of German society, including the majority of the military. The small amount of resistance to the Hitler phenomenon was isolated to very selected parts of the German military and equally insightful and cautious parts of the German intellectual class – many of these individuals being members of the same grouping. It was well known among the German population that if the Goebblels propaganda did not have the desired effect, then the SS re-education camps would. This situation so established in German society assured a condition whereby Adolf Hitler would be identified as a religious German savior by an ever increasing number of people, year by year, as the Nazi educated German youth matured and took their places as authorities in the new *society of supermen*. The Nazi hierarchy could clearly see a time in the immediate future when Adolf Hitler would be universally idealized and accepted as a leader of the new German religion and the deified Savior of the German people. The fact that Hitler decided to attack the Soviet Union in May of 1941, is unexplainable, except by understanding that in late 1940 Hitler saw himself as the Savior of the German people, sent by God, himself, and would lead a religious conquest of the godless, Jewish-led USSR, much as was done in the earlier Crusades, but with considerably more cultural and military effect. So much success and popular adoration had caused him, finally, to start believing his own propaganda. He had forgot the old Roman admonition that *all fame is fleeting.*

The fundamental thesis of this book, that Adolf Hitler *was a religionist* and saw himself in that role, is supported by a great amount of historical literature, which subsumes the contention of the author without explicitly stating it. To support this claim quotations from a representative sample of four books written about Adolf Hitler and his Nazi regime will be made.

Nazi Germany 1933 – 1945, Faith and Annihilation, by Jost Dulffer.

1. Page 14. Indeed, in 1925 Joseph Goebbels placed Hitler on a level with the founder of the Christian religion: "I read Hitler's book from cover to cover, with rapacious excitement! Who is this man? Half plebeian, half god! Really the Christ, or only John the Baptist?" (14 October 1925).

2. Page 15. As such a mass longing became focused on one man. Hitler himself accepted the adoration shown him and identified himself more and more with it.

3. Page 15. But probably only after the 1920s had Hitler, who gave the impression of a rather unpolished man when he appeared socially, gained the certainty that he was not just a prophet making straight the way for some other national leader, but that he should fulfill that role himself. In 1932 he was still flirting only tactically with the term "drummer boy". Although Germany's acceptance of a doctrine of salvation as a political programme had deep causes within its society, it was not clear at the very beginning that Hitler himself would become the embodiment of such a programme.

4. Page 87. We have already pointed out the religious aspects of the cult centered around and in Hitler as an individual. . . . Unlike the redemption offered by religious traditions, however, the quasi-salvation offered to Germans by National Socialism was to be of this world, would take place in history, and would be achieved by German policies. [The author notes that this sort of "worldly" promise is equivalent in all important ways with that given by Marxism and the USSR, under the leadership first of V.I. Lenin and then Jose Stalin. This seems consistent, since so much of what Hitler proposed and installed in the German society was gleaned from the Soviet Union]

5. Page 88. In Cologne the respected Germanist Ernst Bertram proclaimed, with reference to Holderlin and Goethe, "We have been permitted to experience what too many had forgotten or believed that they could deride: that in a people who have not been abandoned by the spirit of history a great danger will call forth a great salvation, and a great savior."

6. Page 88. Above all, the faith in the Fuhrer affected all classes: students, lawyers and doctors, farmers and industrial workers, artisans and white-collar workers. Hitler became the point of reference and focus of personal loyalty in the integration of German society; and of course, some aspects of this development also had a political content. Many Germans later mentioned the fascination that Hitler exerted over them, in personal conversations with members of the Nazi leadership, in the mass

experience of political rallies and marches. Conversely, those who later describe in detail how the Fuhrer had not exercised any irresistible emotional power over them were surprised to find that their experience was not typical. [The author suggests that this phenomenon may be of individual human Neanderthal/Cro-Magnon component in origin, in both the listener and Hitler]

7. Page 90. But when Hitler appeared as a hero hewn out of stone, and occasionally on the motion-picture screen as a hero among heros or, as in the works of Fritz Erler, in the form of a larger-than-life stone hero armed with an eagle and sword, his much more far-reaching, almost religious claim to leadership was suggested.

8. Page 90. Dulffer quotes Goering as saying, ". . . Today the entire nation, the entire people feels strong and happy, because in you not only the Fuhrer but also the savior of the nation has appeared."

9. Page 91. The discrepancy between the Hitler who was adored with religious fervor and the real person can only be explained by the eagerness to believe, by the will to venerate, which was shared by many Germans as well as by others.

Adolph Hitler: A Family Perspective, by Helm Stierlin.

1. Page 79. . . . he had to link the notion and myth of the German nation as mother to other supporting notions and myths. To this end, he had to delve further into the intermediate area. And this he did, as M. Eliade (1972), for one, has shown, by appropriating myths that people have shared throughout history. These included the myth that good and evil, dark and fair, eternally fight each other; that the chosen – i.e., the strong, loyal, and noble ones – enter the kingdom of Heaven, while the damned – i.e., the weak, disloyal, and slavish ones – must perish; and that there exists, somewhere, somehow, a Jerusalem, a sacred mother-city that requires holy war and sacrifice.

2. Page 111. For faith, according to Hitler, "Is harder to shake than knowledge, love succumbs less to change than respect, hate is more enduring than aversion, and the impetus to the mightiest upheavals on this earth has at all times consisted less in a scientific knowledge dominating the masses than in a fanaticism which

inspire them and sometimes in a hysteria which drove them forward."

3. Page 111. Hence, he concludes: "From the army of often millions of men . . . *one* man must step forward who with apodictic force will form granite principles from the wavering idea-world of the broad masses and take up the struggle for their sole correctness, until from the shifting waves of a free thought-world there will arise a brazen cliff to solid unity in faith and will."

4. Page 113. In the pairing group, they strive to create something, some hope, some new idea or Messiah through a pair that is recruited *from*, and – to use my concept – delegated *by* the group. In the oneness group, they "seek to join in a powerful union with an omnipotent force, unobtainably high, to surrender self for passive participation, and thereby to feel existence, well-being and wholeness." [This is a method for many individuals to gain psychological visibility.]

5. Page 115. Finally, we observe such group fantasies to operate in religious and ideological movements, in that these often represent early infantile part objects. Frequently the imagery of these part objects implies primitive, i.e., preoedipal, ambivalence or denial. Thus, the church stands for the good, flowering breast, the virgin for the unbloody vagina, the witch for the bad, poisonous breast, Christ for the killed yet living son, God for the infanticidal yet devine Father, the "Capitalist" (to the Community) for the exploitative, controlling mother, the "Communist" (to the capitalist) for the raging baby.

No doubt, these ideas can throw light on Hitler's relations with Germany. For, like Freud's group theory, they provide conceptual tools to grasp the fit between Hitler's and the German people's contributions. For example, in the framework Hitler's "unerring certainty and power of will" matches a group expectancy (or fantasy) of dependence and oneness, his hammering away at the Jews matches one of "fight/flight" (i.e. serves to "split off" and control the group's projected violence), and his pose of God-like omnipotence matches the group's underlying fear of abandonment.

*   *   *

Stierlin proposes three myths for families that he applies to Hitler's program vis-a-vis the German people. These are *family harmony, exculpation and redemption*, and *salvation*. And these are, indeed, myths, that require an exercise of faith in order to be believed.

*   *   *

6. Page 121. For he espoused, first, a myth of harmony, envisioning *one Folk* that, relieved of all inner strife and totally "ausgerichtet", spoke with one voice, felt with one heart, and marched to one tune. He espoused, second, a myth of exculpation and redemption, *wherein one victim-delegate, the Jew, exculpated all other members and thus cemented their harmony* [italics by the author]; and he espoused, third, a myth of salvation that required him, Adolf Hitler, to act as Germany's lone savior. [This was Hitler's plan for creating a whole society to which he could "belong." He would not (could not) change – the German people had to.]
7. Page 127. They [the German people] wanted to have a guiding principle that one could defer to without further ado, without reflecting on his deeds and considering whether something is correct or false.

*   *   *

These last quotations point to a recurrent theme in many of the German interviews: the anguish of ambiguity, the pain of deciding among alternatives. Ambiguity begets confusion, and confusion is an internal state most deeply feared. Out of the fear of ambiguity, and the deeper fear of confusion, of being adrift in a sea of possibilities, comes the need to reduce diversity, to seek order, clarity, and direction. Hence the German youngster turns to the strong leader. Without firm leadership, there will be chaos, anarchy.

Meta-Politics The Roots of the Nazi Mind,
by Peter Viereck.

1. Page xxii. [Viereck quotes Adolf Hitler's boyhood friend, August Kubicek.] Richard Wagner's music dreams were still the object o four undivided love and enthusiasm. For Adolf, nothing could

compete with the great mystical world that the Master conjured up for us . . . He no longer felt lonely and outlawed, and misjudged by society. He was intoxicated and bewitched. Willingly he let himself be carried away into that mystical universe which was more real to him than the actual workaday world. [This observation by Viereck sets the psychological and philosophical state in the mind and active thoughts of Adolf Hitler that remained fundamental in the man to his death in 1945.]

2. Page xxiv. Mussolini's fascist imperialism, never fully totalitarian, lacked the Aryan blood-cult basic to Hitler-Wagner and was far less "socialist", collectivized, or organic. . . . Germany's deliberate anti-rational religion of organic folk and blood is not the same as statism, although including statism; in contrast Soviet statism and Italian-fascist statism seem mechanical, bureaucratic, and at least relatively rational.

3. Page xxvi. Richard Wagner, product of the German romantic school and of the Jahn-influenced student movement, was to the Nazi revolution – even though less completely and less explicitly – what Rousseau was to the French Revolution and Marx to the Russian Revolution. Rousseau would have been horrified by Robespierre; Marx by Stalin; Wagner by Hitler. [In this quote Viereck captures both the source and the essence of the Naziism of the 1930s. It has been said that the event of Naziism would have been impossible without Adolf Hitler; and that is true. It is also true that the extyreme emotionalism of Wagner's music and the extreme nationalism of his philosophy was combined with the romantic mythology permeating the contemporary Weimar society, and distilled through the medium of Adolf Hitler into the cultural forcing function he used to drive the radical elements of the Nazi movement into popular acceptance by the German public. This acceptance was done on the basis of a religious styled faith, since the rational construct of the published Nazi philosophy, from Rosenberg (Hitler's teacher), Goebbels, and Hitler, himself, was so poor as to be embarrassing to critical examination. This is exemplified by the Nazi party's "25 Points," issued in 1920.]

4. Page 5. Nazism (sic) stands for the opposite of each of these three heritages [rationalism, classicism, Christianity]: for force against reason, for romanticism, for tribal paganism.
5. Page 6. [Viereck quotes Fichte as] ". . . the Germans understand by Kultur an intimate union between themselves and the natural forces of the Universe, . . . :[This is the "culture" that Hitler built his Nazi religion upon and it is *strongly* "Neanderthal".]
6. Page 9. [Viereck quotes H. S. Chamberlain as] " . . . it is the war of modern mechanical "civilization" against the elemental old holy, eternally reborn "Kultur" of superior races."
7. Page 136. In fact, his premonitions of his "approaching death," revealed by members of his entourage and by his own speech of September 1, 1939, suggest that for him this war is a grand Wagnerian Gotterdamerung (Twilight of the Gods) with the whole of Europe afire as a funeral pyre for Adolf Hitler.
8. Page 283. In 1937 Germany's Protestant leaders wished to attend the international Christian conference at Oxford, expressing the indivisibility of world Christianity. The German government forbade its Protestant pastors to attend. It fiercely attacked them in *The Black Corps*, official magazine of Hitler's S.S. bodyguards and tolerant to the pre-Christian pagan cults.
9. Page 285. Rosenberg's religious views stem directly from the following aphorisms by his "great German dreamer", Lagarde: "For every nation, a national religion is necessary."
10. Page 286. [Viereck quotes Rosenberg as] . . . that the so-called Old Testament must be *abolished* officially. Ever more Nazi educators of the young follow his advice to replace instruction in the Old Testament by "nordic sagas from Wotan on."
11. Page 287. Even lip-service to Jesus is scorned by those Nazis who worship the pre-Christian gods like Wotan, popularized by Wagner's Siegried dramas. Nazi bookshops often teem with heathen books and newspapers. Christian Easter coincides with an old heathen spring festival, and Nazi heathen have been granted facilities for public Easter celebrations of their own. These celebrations have substituted for Christian songs the Song of the Goths: "Up the Viking banner, up the blue sun-flat."

12. Page 287. His [Baldur von Schirack] beloved German youth he indoctrinates with Rosenberg, with worship of the old heathen warriors, and with religious faith in Hitler as the New Messiah.

13. Page 288. Two examples will suffice to show how the three Hegelian concepts are translated into Nazi paganism. A founder of the "German Christian Church" told a Berlin mass meeting that "the Nazi state" supersedes the churches because it "*embodies* the totality of God." And Pastor Leffler's book *Christ in the Third Reich*, asks the world to "choose between Israel and Germany" as to which is the "chosen people" to embody the "God of history." Hitler is the new "Savior whom God sent." Unlike Christ, this new Savior is not sent to humanity as a whole but – an important Nazi distinction! – to Germany alone. "This is our faith: after two thousand years the Eternal has summoned the Germans to fulfill the mission that He laid in the cradle of the race.

14. Page 288. Once German universities were world-famous for their spirit of scientific inquiry. Today a tablet in Munich University quotes the creed of [Robert] Ley, the Labor-Front Fuhrer. Ley's creed: Hitler is his religion and Naziism his faith; students should not seek to understand Hitler with their mere intellects but "with their hearts," in religious faith. In speeches to his labor unions Ley even more frankly makes Hitler god.

15. Page 289. Ley said to fifteen thousand Hitler-Youths in 1937: "We believe on this earth *solely* in Adolf Hitler. We believe that National Socialism is the *sole* faith and salvation of our people. We believe that God has sent us Adolf Hitler."

16. Page 289. Dr. Engelke, a "German Christian," has said: "God has manifested himself not in Jesus Christ but in Adolf Hitler."

17. Page 289. . . . . but Kerrl [Hanns] had proceeded to actual deification: "As Christ in his twelve disciples raised a stock fortified unto martyrdom, so in Germany today we are experiencing the same thing . . . Adolf Hitler is the true Holy Ghost." [The author notes that this was not meant as an analogy.]

18. Page 289. ". . . was best summed up in Baldur von Schirack's boast of his German youth movement: "I am neither a Catholic nor a Protestant: I am a National Socialist."

19. Page 290. An old-fashioned German death-notice reads: "died in belief in God." Today newspapers sometimes carry as death-notice: "died in belief in Adolf Hitler."

20. Page 290. For example, seven hundred pastors were arrested in Prussia in one fell swoop in 1935 for denouncing modern paganism from the pulpit.

21. Page 292. Rosenberg says: "Wotan, as the eternal mirror of the primeval soul-forces of the nordic man, is living today as five thousand years ago."

22. Page 293. The Germanic craves a pantheistic God identified with romantic "force of nature"; the Semitic and Christian craves the "other-worldly God." The Germanic craves the salvation of the Volk as an organic whole; the Semitic and Christian craves "salvation of the *individual*."

    The Germanic craves a hair-on-the-chest "heroic ethics"; the Semitic and Christian craves an ethics of peace. Therefore "we of the German religion demand" that this new religion be taught in the schools instead of "Christian instruction," which should be regarded as "no longer a religion."

23. Page 298. One of these very young German aviators was shot down in France and dying. A priest crept to him under a bombardment to offer the last Christian comforts. The dying boy replied: "The Fuhrer is my faith. I don't want anything from your church. But if you want to be good to me, get my Fuhrer's picture out of my breast pocket." The priest got it. The boy kissed the picture, with the usual beatific expression attributed to Christian saints and martyrs, and murmured: "My Fuhrer, I am happy to die for you."

24. Page 300. What Hitler deem the "new" religious force of nazism (sic) is the oldest of all forces. It is not so much anti-Christian as pre-Christian, as old as Cain, as old as the terrible starkness of nature before Christianity came to tame and restrain nature.

25. Page 300. The discussion of this new-old Nazi religion is best closed with an old warning to the better half of Germany and to the west. This old warning was voiced prophetically by the poet Heine more than a century ago. . . . "These doctrines," wrote Heine in 1834, "have developed revolutionary forces which only

await the day to break forth and fill the world with terror and astonishment." . . . The Christian Cross has for centuries kept tame "that brutal German joy in battle," but Heine concluded: "Should the subduing talisman, the Cross, break, then will come roaring forth the wild madness of the old champions, the insane Berserker rage, of which the northern poets sing. That talisman is brittle, and the day will come when it will pitifully break. The old stone gods will arise from the long-forgotten ruin and rub the dust of a thousand years from their eyes; and Thor, leaping to life with his giant hammer, will crush the Gothic cathedrals!"

*   *   *

This last quote of Heine's is a sterling description of the ever-emerging unstable hybrid that is modern man – the Cro-Magnon component in the modern human being (the insane Berzerker rage). This chapter deals with the intimate religious nature of the Nazi movement, and the man who started it. Adolf Hitler, without ever knowing the fundamental genetic source of his psychological drive, was using the power of the religious effect in Mankind to consolidate and control the Cro-Magnon component of (formerly) greatly superior physical prowess in the population of Germany. The age-old method of the Neanderthal religious power was being (successfully) used by a modern "Neanderthal", Adolf Hitler, to shackle the Cro-Magnon component of modern man, much as it must have been done 35,000 YBP with pure Cro-Magnon in what is now modern Israel and Iraq. In Ayn Rand's characterization, this is a case of the Witch Doctor endeavoring to control Attila. In these terms, the case for ascribing religious component to the Neanderthal (and to Naziism, a "Neanderthal" movement) is a good one. Neanderthal **means** religion.

Adolf Hitler The Psychopathic God,
by Robert G. L. Waite.

1. Page 27. Since Hitler saw himself as a Messiah with a devine mission to save Germany from the incarnate evil of "International Jewery," it is not surprising that he likened himself to Jesus. On

one occasion during the 1920s, as he lashed about him with the whip he habitually carried, he said that "in driving out the Jew I remind myself of Jesus in the temple." At another time he said, "Just like Jesus, I have a duty to my own people . . ."

2. Page 27. Christ had changed the dating of history; so would Hitler, for his final victory over the Jews would mark the beginning of a new age in the history of the world. "What Christ began," he observed, he, Hitler, "would complete." And in a speech on 10 February 1933 he parodied the Lord's Prayer in promising that under him a new kingdom would come on earth, and that his would be "the power and the glory, Amen."

3. Page 27. He told an aide that during the preceding autumn [1919], as he lay wounded in a military hospital, he had received a supernatural vision which commanded him to save Germany.

4. Page 28. That he saw himself as the special agent of God and identified with Him was made manifest on many occasions: [Hitler quote] I believe that it was God's will that from here (Austria) a boy was sent into the Reich and that he grew up to become a leader of the nation.

5. Page 28. On one occasion an aide noted that "God doe snot let people look at the cards he holds" [Der liebe Gott laast sich nicht in seine carten sehen]. Hitler immediately broke forth in such a paroxysm of fury that he himself feared a heart attack. He gave orders that the aide never repeat the offensive phrase.

6. Page 28. In as speech in his home town of Linz, 12 March 1938: "When I once departed from this city, I carried with me the very same confession of faith that fills me today . . . . If Providence once then called me from out of this city . . . then Providence must thereby have given me a mission . . . ."

7. Page 28. After the failure of the bomb plot of 20 July 1944 he took a naval aide, 'Now the Almighty has stayed their (assassins') hands once more. Don't you agree that I should consider it as a nod of Fate that it intends to preserve me for my assigned task." His valet remembers that Hitler was very calm, saying, "That is new proof that I have been selected from among other men by Providence to lead greater Germany to victory." And again,

"Because I have been saved while others had to die, it is clearer than ever that the fate of Germany lies in my hands."

8. Page 29. His version of human history was essentially one of religious mythology. He believed that a pure German people had lived in an early Garden of Eden. But this pure race had been attacked by the Devil, made incarnate in the form of the Jew. Indeed he said explicitly that "the Jew is the personification of the Devil and of all evil." And thus he reached his conclusion that in fighting the Devil he was doing the work of Almighty God.

9. Page 29. He did not view the Party and the Reich merely as secular organizations. "I consider those who establish or destroy a religion much greater than those who establish a State, to say nothing of founding a Party," he had written in Mein Kampf. And years later he told his followers, "We are not a movement, rather we are a religion."

10. Page 29. The institutional pattern he used for creating his New Order was the Roman Catholic Church, which had so greatly impressed him. As a boy he had dreamed of being an abbot. When he became Fuhrer, however, he raised his sights and saw himself as a political Pope with an apostolic succession. He announced to a closed meeting of the faithful in the Brown house during 1930: "I hereby set forth for myself and my successors in the leadership of the Party the claim of political infallibility. I hope the world will grow as accustomed to that claim as it has to the claim of the Holy Father.

11. Page 29. He also fancied himself as a religious leader of the non-Christian world he planned to conquer. "I'm going to become a religious figure. Soon I'll be the great chief of the Tartars. Already Arabs and Moroccans are mingling my name with their prayers." [It is noteworthy that this is still happening in modern times.]

12. Page 29. Hitler was striking parallels between his Ministry of Propaganda and Enlightenment and the church's Congregation for the Propaganda of the Faith (Congregatio de Propaganda Fide). He remarked that his task was not to communicate knowledge "but holy conviction and unconditional faith." He viewed the 25 articles of his Party as "the dogma of our faith" and the "rock"

upon which the Party was built. Hitler's proclamation of the "Thousand Year Reich" has religious resonance. He was also fond of speaking of the inseparable Trinity" of State, Movement, and *Volk*. As the sign and symbol of his movement Hitler chose a special type of cross, and personally modified the design of this *Hakenkreuz*.

13. Page 30. As Albert Speer has noted, "It was basically a hall of worship [the colossal Assembly Hall planned for the new Berlin of the future]. . . . without such cult significance the motivation for Hitler's main structure would have been senseless and unintelligible."

14. Page 30. "Above all, I have learned from the Jesuit order." Certainly the oath of direct obedience to the Fuhrer was strikingly reminiscent of the special oath that Jesuits swear to the Pope. Moreover, Hitler spoke of his elite SS, who wore the sacred symbol and dressed in black, as his Society of Jesus. *He also ordered SS officers to study the Spiritual Exercises of Ignatius Loyola for training in the rigid discipline of the faith.* [the author's italics]

15. Page 30. The close parallel between commitment to God and the sacred oath of allegiance to Hitler is seen in a description of public oath-taking recorded in the Nazi newspaper *Westdeutcher Beobachter*: "Yesterday witnessed the profession of the religion of the blood in all its imposing reality . . . whoever has sworn his oath of allegiance to Hitler has pledged himself unto death to this sublime idea."

16. Page 30. The bolts of excommunication and anathema which Hitler hurled against nonbelievers and heretics were not unlike those of a Gregory VII: "Woe to them who do not believe. These people have sinned . . . *sinned* against all of life . . . it is a miracle of faith that Germany has been saved. Today more than ever it is the duty of the Party to remember this National Socialist confession of faith [Galubensbekenntnis] and to bear it forward as our holy [heiliges] sign of our battle and our victory."

17. Page 30. The Nazis, like the Catholics, had their prophets, saints, and martyrs. The Fuhrer sanctified his disciples who fell during the Beer Hall Putsch when he said, in dedicating their memorial,

that their death would begin forth "a true belief in the resurrection of their people . . . the blood that they shed becomes the baptismal water of the Third Reich."

18. Page 30. Hitler's holy reliquary was the Brown House, containing the sacred Blood Flag which had been borne by the martyrs of 9 November 1923. It was Hitler and Hitler alone who could perform the priestly ritual of touching the Blood Flag to the standards of the Brown Shirts.

19. Page 31. Hitler also provided the holy scriptures for his new religion, and *Mein Kampf*, instead of the Bible, took the place of honor in the homes of thousands of German families. With a lack of humor typical of the regime, the Nazis chose this title to replace the prayer book as the appropriate wedding gift for young couples.

20. Page 31. The parallel between Hitler and the Messiah was made explicit in German schools. On 16 March 1934 children wrote out the following dictation approved by Hitler's Ministry of Enlightenment and Propaganda. "Jesus and Hitler. As Jesus freed men from sin and hell, so Hitler freed the German people from destruction. Jesus and Hitler were persecuted, but while Jesus was crucified Hitler was raised to the Chancellorship . . . . Jesus strove for Heaven, Hitler for the German earth."

21. Page 31. The League of German Girls developed a new version of the Lord's Prayer which was a supplication not only *for* the Fuhrer but to him as a deity: "Adolf Hitler, you are our great leader. Thy name makes the enemy tremble. Thy Third Reich comes, thy will alone is law upon the earth. Let us hear daily thy voice and order us by thy leadership, for we will obey to the end even with our lives. We praise thee! Heil Hitler!"

22. Page 31. And smaller children were taught to use this grace before meals: "Fuhrer, my Fuhrer, sent to me from God, protect and maintain me throughout my life. Thou who hast saved Germany from deepest need, I thank thee today for my daily bread. Remain at my side and never leave me, Fuhrer, my Fuhrer, my faith, my light. Heil my Fuhrer!

23. Page 32. In public speech and private soliloquy, and in ways in which he may not have been aware, Hitler himself spoke the

very words of Christ and the scriptures. In talking to his Brown Shirts on 30 January 1936 he echoed the words of Jesus to his disciples as recorded in St. John's Gospel, saying, "I have come to know thee. Who thou art, thou art through me and all I am I am through thee." He reminded one of his disciples that "I have come to Germany not to bring peace but a sword." In a public speech in Graz in 1938 he used the words of Jesus as recorded by Matthew when he announced that Almighty God had created the Nation, "and what the Lord has joined together let not Man set asunder."

24. Page 32. He was particularly prone to Biblical quotations when talking to his Hitler Youth. On 5 September 1934 he told them, "You are flesh of our flesh and blood of our blood." In 1932 he advised them either to be "hot or cold, but lukewarm should be damned and spewed from your mouth." The phrasing is too close to the New Testament to be coincidental. The Book of Revelation (3:15-16) reads: "I know thy works. Thou are neither cold nor hot; I would thou wert cold or hot. So then because thou art lukewarm, and neither cold nor hot, I will spew thee out of my mouth."

25. Page 32. He was fond of calling for a faith that could move mountains, saying on 31 January 1935, "If you had not had faith, who could have led thee? Faith can remove mountains, can free also nations." And in May of the same year, speaking about faith, he reminded the faithful. "It is the strength which in the end can remove the mountains of resistance!" [Waite compares this quotation with I Corinthians 13:2.]

26. Page 32. During one of his last suppers with his followers when he invited them to partake of their Leader's body by eating blood sausage made from his own blood, was he not saying, "Take, eat: this is my body which is broken for you . . . "?

Based on the previous quotations and on a detailed philosophical examination of Nazi doctrine, the author makes the claim that Naziism was a religion in all important ways – the religion of Adolf Hitler, created by him and accepted by a majority of the people of Germany. And the author observes that (given the evidence) this claim is quite beyond question. He further points out to the reader that the Nazi religion is philosophically virtually identical to all religions, historical and modern. This evaluation applies markedly, to modern Christianity. The *fundamental* operative difference between the Christianity of today and the Naziism of 1940, is the power gained by the political institutionalization of Naziism, and that alone. If modern Christianity (or Islam) ever gains political institutionalization, as did Naziism in the 1930s, the American (and western) public will find themselves recoiling in horror at being subjected to the age-old terror and monstrousness that religion, in power, has always forced upon Mankind. *Reason and the intellectual liberation of the* **Enlightenment** *really is that important.*

CHAPTER 8

Modern Religion And Naziism:
The Obvious Parallels

Religions, all across the world, have a remarkable press. It seems that no matter what happens on the world stage, if the actions can be said to occur in the name of religion, all is allowed, all is judged as good, and all is somehow forgiven. This sanction has begun to develop cracks only in very recent times when it has become apparent even to many hard-over, Christian religionists that there does exist a large and powerful world religion (Islam), whose core philosophy leads them to perform innumerable and unbelievable aggressive horrors against the innocent. But even this religious terror, led by people who claim that Muslims love death (the most despicable and anti-human morality imaginable), is excused and papered-over by western religious pundits and guilty, politically correct "post moderns" who reason that the religion, itself, it not evil, but only the people who carry out its most basic and important religious teachings of Jihad against the western values of individual liberty. Such specious reasoning would not be acceptable in a class of 5th graders, so it seems conclusive that the "reasoning" process these people use is substantiated, mainly, by evasion. It does remain that Islam is the most vicious and immoral social movement in modern times. The trillions of dollars of wealth that has flowed into the coffers of the Saudi royal family has certainly not remained there to attract the dust of the ages. The Saudis, the greatest, richest, and most powerful enemy of Americanism and individual liberty on earth, have funded the spread of the most virulent, malevolent, and malignant form of Islam around the entire globe – Wahhabiism. For western values to survive in the world, Islam (and specifically the Wahhabi sect) must be dealt with, and the method of confrontation must be direct, forceful, and easy for all to understand. In modern parlance, it must be "in your face". Islam was created after Christianity had existed for some 650 years. In the development and accommodation of the religion into a civil movement in comport with the modern facts of reality, it has a long way to go, by comparison. One only has to recall what another major western religion, Christianity, was like in the year 1350 in Mediaeval Europe to understand the place, condition, and attitude of Islam in the modern world.

Historically, the most horrid evils that can be imagined by the human mind were performed against helpless people by and for religions across the entire world. This philosophical outlook and these disgusting actions continued to be forced on societies, even in the Western world, until their gradual de-institutionalization over some 200 years, from the middle of the 18th Century to the middle of the 20th Century. In modern times, the horrors of institutionalized religion are limited to the more primitive peoples of the earth, for the most part in the Middle East, areas of the Far East, and on the African Continent.

But the destructive effects of the Christian religion are still important, even in the United States, possessing the most secular governmental system of any size on the world stage. An examination of the fundamentals of religion in this country will now be undertaken and a comparison of those fundamentals made with the social/philosophical system established by Adolph Hitler – institutionalized in the 1930s German government as the National Socialist Worker's Party of Germany – the Nazis.

Religious Fundamentals

All religions, that can truly be classed as religions, have several fundamentals in common. These are, 1) a belief in the supernatural, 2) the requirement of "faith" in the convert, 3) a belief in the religion's creed, 4) a belief in the temporal leader(s) of the religion, and 5) financial support of the religion and its leadership by the convert. The actual, esoteric purpose of items number 1,2,3 and 5 above are to support the directions and the programs of the religion's leader(s). Truly, if there were no real-time activity of the religion promoted and driven by the religion's leadership, the religion would not, in fact, exist. That is, the religion and its leadership, to exist at all, requires a program and method of operation alive and functioning within its containing society to provide it with its reason for being, for both convert and leader alike.

As much as it claims to exist for purposes of the supernatural or the infinite, religion (all religions and their leaders) completely depend upon and exist within the physical world and the facts of reality as so well defined by modern science and the scientific method. Religion's claim for and dependence upon the ineffable are, cart blanch, non-veridical.

Nazi Fundamentals

Naziism, like most modern religions, had its temporal and geographic roots in an area in which the people were socially unsettled and threatened. An extraordinarily charismatic political demagogue with extraordinary oratorical skills managed, first, to capture the attention and admiration of a beer cellar, political discussion group named the German Worker's Party, and ultimately transform it into a powerful political movement (the NSDAP, or the National Socialist German Worker's Party) that ended up controlling the nation state of Germany in 1933-34, and all of Europe in 1940. The Nazi party succeeded in consolidating control in Germany by means of, 1) the great faith of the party members in Adolf Hitler, followed in time by that of the German nation, 2) an overwhelming belief by the German people in the Nazi program, generated over the first six years of Hitler's reign, 3) a pervasive acceptance by the German people in the essence of the Nazi "Twenty-Five Point" platform, 4) the (ultimately) strong financial support of a majority of Germans typified by the wealthy industrialists Gustav Krupp and Friz Thyssen, followed finally by, 5) a belief by much of the German public and the almost universal rabid belief by the younger part of the population in the *sacred nature* of Hitler's rule over Germany and his mission in the world. The essence of the Nazi fundamentals matches closely those of the Christian religion formed some 2,000 years before, with the charismatic leadership of Jesus of Nazareth (if he was even actually an historical figure) and Paul of Tarsus. There exists an even closer parallel with the formation of Islam some 1350 years ago, and the charismatic leadership of the religious prophet, Mohammed, especially following his first marriage to a wealthy and influential woman of a more advanced age.

Religion in the Modern United States

Religion in the modern United States is a mere shadow of its previous self. The Enlightenment acceptance of the ability of science and the scientific method to explain the questions of the world, and define and organize Man's place in the universe, has destroyed claim after claim by religion as authoritative. Science has marginalized the effect of religion to a small set of "true believers" and a thin, and forever thinning, veneer over the society as a whole. Fewer and fewer people are willing to give even serious lip-service to religious beliefs, and more and more modern thinkers are willing to question the use of faith by people as a justification to belief or action. Reason is finally destroying faith in the Western World and will continue to do so, unless religion-inspired government force is brought to bear against the populace. As always, in modern times, the rest of the world follows the lead of the United States in things of importance.

But the secondary effects of religion in the American society are not inconsequential. When religious ideas and concepts are ingrained in a society over generations, many of the ramifications of those ideas are incorporated into the everyday living that determines the defacto *terms of association* – the social intercourse – of people as they interact in their daily lives. Indeed, people generally, may not even understand that many of the rules and standards by which they think and live have religious origins. When these rules and standards prove to be rational and defendable by argumentation, they are often simply taken as *common sense*. Then they are not defendable by reason, they are often accepted as, "something everyone believes" or "something my parents taught me".

The man-on-the-street seldom spends the time and effort to identify his personal standards unambiguously, and thus, determine their origins and their veridicality. Such an effort would actually become an identification of one's personal philosophy, or *rules for living*. Of course all individual human beings possess a personal philosophy, which they allow to determine the direction of their lives, but this all important element is rarely examined in any detail, and placed under the bright light of the rational faculty. This tendency carries over into the realm of religious matters, to an extreme.

The respectful non-religious, the non-serious religious, and the hard-over religious fanatic all allow religious matters in their lives to be determined by those in the society who claim to be "experts" in the field and hold a hammerlock on all important things religious. This failure of personal responsibility toward religion in the society is reminiscent of a parallel personal failure toward things political, and results in some of the same types of wrongs and excesses by those in political authority. People say that they pay others to do those sorts of things for them. But it is not always for them that things are so done – not exactly. The result of this inattention is a defacto enslavement of all those in the American society, who do show respect for religion, to those religious pundits whose true purpose is to control the actions and the very thoughts of those around them, for their own emolument. The parallel between things religious and things political referred to above is, in fact, extensive, it is not beneficial, and it is not accidental.

Historically, religion and government have been mutually supporting, even though one important effect of the renaissance was a powerful contest between religious and secular authorities for a more perfect control over people's lives. A certain *reproachmont* was effected between the two competitors that allowed a potent and effective control and subjugation of people by religion, acting through the agencies of state power. This unholy arrangement, made in hell, continued with ever greater strength for several hundred years, in the midieval period, until the early effects of the Enlightenment and the Age of Reason began to dismantle the cooperative effort.

The strongest and most basic effects of the Enlightenment liberation were sidetracked by the influence of the famous philosopher/scientist, Immanuel Kant, in the late 18th Century (a longer discussion follows), and many of the destructive, anti-human consequences of religion again insinuated themselves into the body politic. Even in the 21st Century, in the most secular governmental organization on the planet, the federal American Senate has an opening prayer spoken to a supernatural being, and the very currency with which American citizens are forced by law to accept in economic commerce has an appeal to the supernatural written on it, in the form of, "In God We Trust". In short and in fact, the claim by many pundits that the effects of religion are dead in modern American are greatly exaggerated.

The Survival of Religion

It is perfectly legitimate for a modern human being, living in a heated, air-conditioned house, reading by electrical illumination, and gaining a large amount of his daily information by means of television and the internet, to question why any sort of belief, whatever, is placed in the supernatural, however defined. To provide some sort of coherent answer to this question, one only needs to drift back into history a few hundred years, when the investigation of the natural world and its environment had yet to make much progress.

Only about 500 years ago, the most learned people in the most advanced civilization on earth (in Western Europe) believed the world was flat. Blue-water sailors were warned and made constantly aware of the possibility of sailing off the edge of our flat world, to their destruction (somewhere). These same "learned people" had no idea of why food spoiled, or what caused disease (except evil spirits), or what made the sun shine or the sky blue, but believed, profoundly, that devils and demons could invade a human body and cause havoc, or literally throw people off bridges or towers to their deaths. The richest and most powerful men in Europe could not keep their houses warm in the winter or cool in the summer. Journeys of more than a few tens of miles were major undertakings and medical treatment was a horror few were willing to accept. And it is important to modern understanding to observe that the foregoing cursory description is indicative of a thoroughgoing, common mind-set that saw the world and human existence as unfriendly and non-beneficial – a result of Augustinian philosophical views, and those of the Christian Church. A pervasive supernaturalism, supported strongly by common religion and its teachings permeated every thought and action of the population. The supernatural (to these people) was *real* – as real as the rising sun, and all the important authorities said so; and it would forever remain real (so they said). But there were doubters of the ruling orthodoxy in the world – fuelled by a powerful and growing reliance on the efficacy of rational thought – the doubters we later learned to call scientists and philosophers.

If one takes the Renaissance period as that time in Europe between the 14th and the 16th Centuries, then the condition of religion in the societies of his period ranges, in analogical equivalence, from that of a modern totalitarianism to that of the autarky of a modern Russia. The partial liberation of men's minds in the use of their natural reason by Thomas Aquinas in the middle of the 13th Century, slowly led to a flowering of scientific inquiry in all fields of endeavor, that only increasingly bloomed over the years. It is not that Mankind was suddenly freed from the mental and physical prison of religious dogma (that freedom would not begin to occur until the Enlightenment years of the 18th Century), but the pervasive overburden of a penetrating supernatural ambiance was lifted, partially, to release (among many other beneficial things) that extraordinarily creative economic human power men would later call, capitalism.

Immanuel Kant; Religion, Science, and History

Immanuel Kant was born in Koenigsberg, East Prussia, in 1724. He entered the world at a most pregnant time in history. The powerful religious control over the minds and actions of men had begun to develop large cracks in the late Enlightenment period, as the competition for Man's allegiance between sacred and secular authority heated up. These "cracks" were actually openings for the men of outstanding intellect (and others) who have forever hammered at the ceilings of intellectual and physical restraint placed on the whole of society by the authority of government (both secular and sacred) which desired to control the actions of men who did not accept its own view of the proper and the moral.

Kant was a deep thinker and a philosopher, who developed ideas and opinions at variance with the then current orthodoxy. He was simply too good at using his mind in the rational way to swallow (entirely) the philosophical jumble that composed the system of laws, rules, and prohibitions of his intellectual environment. Thus, he was often at odds with the theocratically minded ruling clique of the Germany of the middle and late 1700s. But Kant was also a man of his own times. He was raised in a religious environment, as was essentially everyone in that place and that period, and imbued with religious beliefs from childhood. In spite of being a profound thinker and philosophical innovator of world class, he still found himself wrapped around the axel of religion on important and fundamental matters.

Immanuel Kant was also a scientist – and a good one, at that. The Kant-Laplace nebular hypothesis of the formation of the solar system does, even by modern standards, properly describe the process of the gravitational accretion of matter to form the sun, planets, and planetary moons. But thinker or not – scientist or not – Kant could simply not accept the universe without the presence of a supernatural supreme being. Thus, we witness (sadly) a great and creative intellect embarked in a serious and concentrated effort to identify and establish a basic philosophical argument that would limit and circumscribe the efficacy of human reason – and do that at the most fundamental level possible, by an attack on the validity of the human senses. Kant could then make a place for God in the universe – a place that had to be accepted by faith, since he (and many other thinkers of his time and since) were quite aware that any rational underpinning of the concept of God was simply out of the question.

Kant, being the historical intellectual that he was, has had an effect on the 19th and 20th Centuries of a fundamental nature, and that nature is not at all good. More than any other man in history, he was responsible (through his philosophy and his published works) for the destruction of, 1) the Enlightenment idea of the unlimited efficacy of the human mind, and 2) the explosive expansion of the spirit of individual liberty that was the byword of Enlightenment values, in spite of the fact that Kant, himself, was (in contradiction) an individualist. In limiting the efficacy of reason, Kant opened the philosophical door to a Pandora's Box of the most horrible and destructive philosophical and political thoughts, and their subsequent social movements in the history of the world. At a very critical time in the development of philosophical thought, one of philosophy's most powerful contributors had flown the airplane into the ground. Today, at the beginning of the 21st Century, the philosophical, social, artistic, and political wreckage can be seen all around us.

Today, after suffering through the Great Awakening (a fundamental religious movement that swept whole areas of America, and especially New England in the 1740s) and later numerous religious revival periods, people observe that the religious elements formerly present in the American society (circa 1700) are still present, both philosophically and politically. Powerful assaults by modern science have marginalized the "true believers" to a small clique on the fringes of philosophy and the social environment, but a troubling and pervasive claim to a belief in the existence of the supernatural permeates the population in the United States. Responsibility for a large part of this condition can be laid at the feet of the government sponsored and run public school system, which certainly does *not* teach its students to use their minds critically, and reject the supernatural as irrational and unacceptable. But the fundamental and most important part of the responsibility must be placed clearly on the weak and narrow shoulders of modern philosophy.

Modern American Christianity

When surveys are taken and questions asked, a large majority of people in the United States admit to a belief in God. This expressed belief is at best ethereal, since the actual evidence for supporting such a claim – knowledge of religious facts, participation in religious oriented events, parental teaching of religion, financial support of religious organizations, the desire to have religion taught in the schools, etc. – is largely absent. There exist hard-over religionists in the society and there exist hard-over atheists. Neither of these groups represent the source of a filmy, almost transparent concept of a belief in a supreme being by the general public. It almost seems that having been born, possessing a father, and having been (at least partially) raised by that father, the children of an American family continue to desire the comforting thought that there may be the continuing presence of a powerful and a loving father-surrogate, available to help define and assure their places in their personal world-concept. Besides, most American children had been mind-conditioned since birth, with the idea that the concept of God represents *goodness* in a fundamental sense, and they reason that a belief in "goodness" cannot be wrong.

There exist religious sects in America that display actions and teachings in their doctrines that can only be described by the disinterested observer as insanity – a mass insanity, similar to that created and observed in many of Hitler's more "emotionally complete" interactions with his audiences. The screaming, raving, and wild-eyed gesticulations of such audiences in response to Hitler's orations tracks one-on-one with almost identical events in the churches of many modern American religious organizations – many of Negro or mostly Negro membership. Some of these "modern" primitive religious organizations perform (apparently) magical healings of abnormal physical and psychological conditions ranging from the curing of diabetes and schizophrenia to enabling crippled legs to walk. And all this is done merely by the "laying of hands" on the afflicted by the religious leader (who has been granted "power" by a supernatural entity) and an emotional appeal to that god for the healing to occur. These and similar processes are actually seen on the nationwide television screens of the United States. And if the "healing" event fails, the failure is blamed on the lack of will and belief of the subject – *exactly* the reason given by Hitler in the spring of 1945, for the failure of the German people to resist and conquer, essentially, the rest of the world.

There exist religious sects in some of the more economically undeveloped areas in the country that encourage the manual handling of deadly poisonous pit vipers – a scenario supposedly demonstrating a mystical "protection" provided to the true believer by an all-powerful god. In even more unusual circumstances this "proof of a faith in God" actually extended to the playing of "Russian roulette" by selected members of the religious organization. This last "demonstration" is losing its popularity, since unsuccessful participants are eliminated from the "game," and many others are sickened at the sight of human brains being spattered all over the meeting hall, and even some of the congregation. But such "extreme" examples as given above are directly identified, intellectually, with the apparently much more refined "belief in a supernatural being" called God. To repeat, the intellectual principle involved in snake handling, Russian roulette, and the most sophisticated "refined" belief in a supernatural being is identical – the acceptance of the irrational into one's cognitive makeup. Such a fundamental breach of principle (and morality) is encouraged not only by religious pundits but also by American government, which (paradoxically) endeavors to distance itself from anything ostensibly connected with religion.

There will always exist, in human societies, times of uncertainty and peril. Such things are not "the normal" for the residents of an even partially free society. But when the intellectuals (the philosophers) whose job it is to lead the way for society in the realm of thinking, unambiguous identification, critical judgment, and evaluation default on their professional calling, people respond to disaster and the unknown by an appeal to the supernatural to help them in their attempts to explain and console. This will forever be true until and unless modern philosophy regains its feet and its stature and, again, leads the way to truth. The very pregnant question in modern times is, how will our ambitious, amoral, and immoral political leadership use the religiously inspired "faith" that most Americans admit to, to gain and consolidate their hold on the reins of power in the country. Are we starting to see an analogical replay of 1930s Germany? Do we have a "new and improved" Adolf Hitler in our future? Time will surely tell.

Bibliography

Dulffer, Jost. *Nazi Germany 1933-1945*; Arnold, London.

Fest, Joachim C. *Hitler*; Harcourt Brace Jovanovich, Inc., New York.

Gooch, Stan. *The Neanderthal Question*; Wildwood House, Ltd., London.

Gooch, Stan. *Total Man*; Holt, Rinehart and Winston, New York.

Hamann, Brigitte. *Hitler's Vienna*; Oxford University Press, Oxford, England.

Hershmont, Jablow and Lieb, Julian; *A Brotherhood of Tyrants*;

Peikoff, Leonard. *The Ominious Parallels*; Stein and Day, New York.

Schwaab, Edleff H. *Hitler's Mind – A Plunge into Madness*; Praeger, New York.

Stierlin, Helm. *Adolf Hitler: A Family Perspective*; The Psychohistory Press, New York.

Viereck, Peter. *Metapolitics – The Roots of the Nazi Mind*; Capricorn Books, New York.

Waite, Robert G. L. *The Psychopathic God, Adolf Hitler*; Da Capo Press, Inc, New York.

Index

arrested development 3, 22, 25, 31
Berzerker rage 73
Bloch, Dr. Eduard 11
Bolshevik Revolution 17
Braunau, Austria 1
Chaotic Social Wave ix, 14, 16
Drexler, Anton 43
Eckhart, Dietrich 43
emotional orgasm 14
Enabling Act xii
Eva Brown 21
federalism xii
Fichte, Johann Gottlieb (1762-
    1814) ix, 70
Free Corps 34
Friedrich the Great (1712-1786)
    17
Fritsch, Theodor 11, 39
Fuhrerprincip x
Geli Rabaul 21
German Worker's Party 82
Goebbels, Joseph (1897-1945) 24,
    32, 62, 63, 64, 69
Goering, Hermann (1893-1946)
    xi, 46, 66
Guderian, Heinz 18, 28
Halder, Franz von xi, 28
Hapsburg Empire 5, 10
Hegel, Georg W.F. (1770-1831) ix
Hindenburg, Paul von (1847-1934)
    xi, xii, 16, 18, 26, 62, 63
Hitler, Alois (1837-1903) viii, ix

Hitler, Klara Polzl (1860-1907)
    viii, 15
Hugenberg, Alfred (1865-1951) xi
idiosavant 31, 35
Inflation of 1922-23 17, 44, 61
Jahn, (Father) Friedrich Ludwig
    (1778-1852) ix, 17, 69
Jews 3, 6, 9, 10, 11, 42, 56, 61,
    67, 74
Kant, Immanuel (1724-1804) vii,
    17, 84, 86, 87
KDP (German Communist Party)
    17
Kenyapithecus, Ramapithecus 52
Kleist, Henrich Wilhelm ix
Kubicek, August 6, 20, 25, 68
Lagarde, Paul Anton de (1827-
    1891) ix, 70
Langbehn, Julius (1851-1907) ix
Lenin, V. I. (1870-1924) xii, 26,
    49, 65
Leuger, Karl (Vienna mayor) 11
Liebenfels, Georg Lanz von 11,
    39, 40
List, Guido von 11, 39, 40
Lohengrin 15
Ludendorff, Erich (1865-1937) 48
Lutheran 1, 2
Luther, Martin (1483-1546) 1
Man of the Year 63
Manstein, Friz Eric von 37, 82
Marr, Wilhelm ix

Marxists 3, 62
military draft, scientists and engineers 10, 32, 37, 84, 86, 87
Morell, Dr. 30
Munich, Germany 1, 25, 33, 34, 35, 40, 43, 44, 47, 71
Narcissistic viii, ix
National Socialist xi, xii, 35, 42, 43, 44, 46, 71, 76, 81, 82
National Socialist German Workers' Party (NAZIs) ix, xii, 30, 35, 42, 44, 46, 51, 70, 76, 77, 81
Nietzsche, Friedrich (1844-1900) ix
osmosis 13
Papen, Franz von (1879-1969) xi
philosophy x, 11, 12, 13, 14, 16, 18, 26, 39, 40, 43, 69, 80, 83, 87, 88, 90
Protocols of the Elders of Zion 42
psychology 47
Rand, Ayn (1905-1982) 73
Rauschning, Hermann (1887-1961) 32, 49
Reich Constitution 18
Reichstag, German xii, 17
Ribbentrop, Joachim von 26, 91
Ringstrasse 10
Rohm, Ernest (1887-1934) 63
Romanticism, German x, 17, 45, 70
Rosenberg, Alfred (1893-1946) 32, 69, 70, 71, 72
SA xi, xii, 38, 44, 49, 50, 63
Schleicher, General Kurt von (1882-1934) xi
sexuality 1, 2
Siegfried 39
Speer, Albert 25, 31, 76

SS, Adolf Hitler's *Society of Jesus* (Schutz Staffeln) 59, 76
Stalin, Josef (1879-1953) xii, 25, 26, 42, 49, 50, 62, 63, 65, 69
Stefanie 21
Teppischfresser 35
Thirty Years War (1618-1648) 17
Thousand Year Reich 4, 76
Versailles Treaty 17
Vienna Art School 7, 21, 40
Vienna, Austria 4, 6, 7, 8, 9, 10, 11, 14, 15, 16, 21, 22, 30, 33, 34, 39, 40, 47, 91
Wagner, Richard (1813-1883) 2, 6, 10, 11, 14, 15, 16, 17, 23, 36, 39, 40, 41, 42, 43, 47, 68, 69, 70
Wahhabi 80
Weber, Max (1881-1961) ix

Printed in the United States
by Baker & Taylor Publisher Services